Aristophanes
Frogs

A new translation and
commentary by Judith Affleck
and Clive Letchford

Introduction to the Greek Theatre
by P.E. Easterling

Series Editors: John Harrison and Judith Affleck

CAMBRIDGE
UNIVERSITY PRESS

CAMBRIDGE
UNIVERSITY PRESS

University Printing House, Cambridge CB2 8BS, United Kingdom

One Liberty Plaza, 20th Floor, New York, NY 10006, USA

477 Williamstown Road, Port Melbourne, VIC 3207, Australia

4843/24, 2nd Floor, Ansari Road, Daryaganj, Delhi – 110002, India

79 Anson Road, #06–04/06, Singapore 079906

Cambridge University Press is part of the University of Cambridge.

It furthers the University's mission by disseminating knowledge in the pursuit of
education, learning and research at the highest international levels of excellence.

Information on this title: www.cambridge.org/9780521172578

© Cambridge University Press 2014

First published 2014

20 19 18 17 16 15 14 13 12

Printed in Great Britain by CPI Group (UK) Ltd, Croydon CR0 4YY

A catalogue record for this publication is available from the British Library

ISBN 978-0-521-17257-8 Paperback

....

Contents

Preface   iv

Background to the story of *Frogs*   v

Short bibliography   viii

Maps of Attica and Athens   ix–x

List of characters   1

Commentary and translation   2

Synopsis of the play   104

Introduction to the Greek Theatre   108

Time line   112

Index   114

Acknowledgements   117

Preface

The aim of the series is to enable students to approach classical plays with confidence and understanding: to discover the play within the text.

The translations are new. Many versions of Greek drama have been produced by poets and playwrights who do not work from the original Greek. The translators of this series aim to bring readers, actors and directors as close as possible to the playwrights' actual words and intentions: to create translations which are faithful to the original in content and tone, and which can be spoken with all the immediacy of modern English. Comedy presents a slightly different set of challenges and compromises for the translator than tragedy does; some of these are discussed in the accompanying notes.

The notes are designed for students of Classical Civilisation and Drama, and indeed anyone who is interested in theatre. They address points which present difficulty for the reader of today, chiefly relating to the Greeks' religious and moral attitudes, their social and political life, and mythology. Our hope is that students should discover the play for themselves. The conventions of the classical theatre are discussed, but there is no thought of recommending 'authentic' performances. Different groups will find different ways of responding to each play. The best way of bringing alive an ancient play, as any other, is to explore the text practically, to stimulate thought about ways of staging the plays today. Stage directions in the text are minimal, and the notes are not prescriptive; rather they contain questions and exercises which explore the dramatic qualities of the text. Bullet points introduce suggestions for discussion and analysis; open bullet points focus on more practical exercises.

If this series encourages students to attempt a staged production, so much the better. But the primary aim is understanding and enjoyment.

This translation of *Frogs* is based on the Greek text edited by N.G. Wilson for the Oxford University Press (2007). The line numbers correspond as far as possible to the original Greek. This explains slight anomalies in the line numbering, where some compression or expansion has taken place in translation. Greek has two different letters for 'e' and 'o' and, where Greek words have been transliterated (using italics), we have marked the longer vowels as ē and ō.

John Harrison
Judith Affleck

Background to the story of **Frogs**

Frogs was produced in Athens early in 405 BC. The Peloponnesian War, between Athens, Sparta and their allies (431–404 BC), ended 18 months later. In the summer of 404 BC Athens accepted as terms of defeat the reduction of her navy to twelve ships, the destruction of the 7 km long walls between the city and harbour at Piraeus, and an end to democratic government. Defeat had not been a foregone conclusion despite huge Athenian losses in the Sicilian Expedition of 415–413 BC. Twice the Spartans had sued for peace: in 410 BC, after the Battle of Cyzicus; and in 406 BC, after the Athenian victory at Arginusae. On both occasions their overtures were rejected through the influence of democrats such as Cleophon, mentioned three times in this play (see p. 100).

Frogs was written and produced at a time of extreme uncertainty. Months before the victory at Arginusae, Athens had suffered severe defeats at the hands of the Spartan commanders Lysander and Callicratidas, and had been forced to take extreme measures to make good the losses: gold and silver from dedications on the Acropolis were melted down to make coins for a new navy and the metal content was adulterated; for the first time slaves were recruited as rowers and possibly rewarded with citizenship. References to both these controversial policies are to be found in this play (see 34n and p. 50). Even victory brought recriminations: after Arginusae the stormy weather prevented members of the fleet from picking up the dead and dying. In a violent reaction, the Athenian assembly voted that all eight generals should be collectively condemned for their failure. The trial took place towards the end of October, when Aristophanes would have been working on the play. Six of the eight were killed, one of whom, Erasinides, is the butt of a bleak joke in line 1196.

The political question that emerges most insistently in this play is whom to trust. The Athenian aristocrat Alcibiades contributed more than his fair share to mixed feelings of mistrust, despair and relief, as Athens lurched between victory and catastrophe and was rent by factions. A prime mover and elected one of the generals of the expedition to Sicily in 415 BC, Alcibiades defected to Sparta to avoid trial for the alleged profanation of the Mysteries and mutilation of statues of Hermes. On his advice, the Spartans garrisoned a permanent fort at Decelea in Attica (see map, p. ix). Alcibiades also played a key part in bringing Persia into the war on the side of Athens' enemies. An affair with the wife of Agis, the Spartan king stationed at Decelea, then contributed to a break with Sparta, and Alcibiades used his wit and resources to charm the Athenians once again. He was pardoned, welcomed, and elected general in 407 BC, until defeat by Lysander at the Battle of Notium in 406 BC led to his replacement (see 'Round 5', p. 96). At the time of *Frogs* he was living in self-imposed exile in his fortress on the Hellespont. Bafflement at how to treat him is evident from the climax to the poetic contest that concludes the play (1422).

Dionysus asks this question after descending into the underworld on a mission to bring back to life a playwright. Athens' three greatest tragic poets, **Aeschylus**, **Sophocles** and **Euripides**, had all died by 405 BC, Aeschylus in the mid fifth century (*c*. 456 BC), his younger rivals more recently, *c*. 406 BC. Dionysus, accepting the traditional view that poets teach their audiences a kind of wisdom, is intent on bringing Euripides back from death, rather as Orpheus had attempted to reverse the untimely death of his bride Eurydice or Demeter that of her daughter Persephone. The only serious difficulty Dionysus encounters is uncertainty about whether Euripides is the right poet – would the old-fashioned Aeschylus be preferable to the modern, sophistic Euripides? In whom should the people of Athens put their trust? Which will give wisest instruction?

The first half of *Frogs* is a comic take on an old story – the hero's death-defying journey to the underworld (*katabasis*). Dionysus seeks advice from **Heracles**, who had descended into Hades under orders from King Eurystheus to perform his final labour and drag the three-headed guard-dog Cerberus from his home. Dionysus dresses like him and enquires about his route. This is not the first play in which Dionysus appears or which involves bringing back worthy figures from the past. In a lost comedy called *Demes*, by Aristophanes' rival Eupolis, four dead politicians are brought back to resolve Athens' political problems; in another play by Eupolis an effete Dionysus learns to row, as he does to the musical accompaniment of a chorus of frogs in this play (209–68).

The second half is dominated by a great poetic contest in the underworld presided over by the god of drama himself, Dionysus. The play reflects aspects of its context – the Athenian dramatic festivals that took place between January and March known as the Lenaea and City Dionysia, where the three chosen poets competed. *Frogs* is not unusual in including such a contest. The *agōn* was a set piece in most Athenian drama, taking the form of a debate or trial, modes of public speaking familiar to the Athenians. In *Clouds*, for example, two personified Arguments compete over who should educate an Athenian youth; and in a lost play by Aristophanes' rival, Phrynichus (*The Muses*, placed second after *Frogs* in 405 BC), a poet is put on trial in the *agōn* – so bringing poets on stage is not unique to Aristophanes either. It is difficult to judge how original an author Aristophanes was, but his eleven surviving plays, admired in his lifetime, have delighted and instructed generations of scholars, historians and theatre-goers ever since. *Frogs*, with its mixture of slapstick, nonsense and more serious political, cultural and moral insights, has proved a perennial favourite.

Short bibliography

Aeschylus, *Agamemnon*, ed. P. de May, Cambridge University Press, 2003.

Aeschylus, *Persians*, in *Prometheus Bound and Other Plays*, ed. P. Vellacott, Penguin, 1970.

Aristophanes, *Clouds*, ed. J. Claughton and J. Affleck, Cambridge University Press, 2012.

Aristophanes, *Frogs*, ed. K.J. Dover, Oxford University Press, 1993. (*Also abridged version of 1997 with less focus on issues of the Greek text.*)

Aristophanes, *Frogs*, ed. A.H. Sommerstein, Aris and Philips, 1999.

Aristophanes, *Frogs*, ed. J. Henderson, The Loeb Classical Library, 2002.

Aristophanes, *Frogs and Other Plays*, trans. D. Barrett, Penguin, 1964.

Aristophanes, *Thesmophoriazusae*, in *The Wasps / The Poet and the Women / The Frogs*, trans. D. Barrett, Penguin, 1964.

Bowie, A.M., *Aristophanes: Myth, Ritual and Comedy*, Cambridge University Press, 1996.

Cartledge, P., *Aristophanes and his Theatre of the Absurd*, Bristol Classical Press, 1990.

Connelly, P., *The Ancient City*, Oxford University Press, 1998.

Dover, K.J., *Aristophanic Comedy*, University of California Press, 1972.

Euripides, *Bacchae*, ed. D. Franklin, Cambridge University Press, 2000.

Euripides, *Hippolytus*, ed. B. Shaw, Cambridge University Press, 2007.

Grant, M., *The Routledge Atlas of Classical History*, Routledge, 1994.

Handley, E., 'Comedy', Chapter 12 in *The Cambridge History of Classical Literature*, Volume I, Cambridge University Press, 1985.

Homer, *The Odyssey*, ed. M. Rieu and P. Jones, Penguin, 2003.

Lada-Richards, I., *Initiating Dionysus: Ritual and Theatre in Aristophanes' Frogs*, Clarendon Press, 1999.

Lefkowitz, M.R., *The Lives of the Greek Poets*, Duckworth, 1981.

MacDowell, D.M., *Aristophanes and Athens*, Oxford University Press, 1995.

Revermann, M., *Comic Business: Theatricality, Dramatic Technique, and Performance Contexts of Aristophanic Comedy*, Oxford University Press, 2006.

Robson, J., ed., *Aristophanes: An Introduction*, Duckworth, 2009.

Russo, C., *Aristophanes, an Author for the Stage*, Routledge, 1997.

Segal, E., ed., *Oxford Readings in Aristophanes*, Oxford University Press, 1996.

Silk, M.S., *Aristophanes and the Definition of Comedy*, Oxford University Press, 2002.

Wright, M., *The Comedian as Critic: Greek Old Comedy and Poetics*, Bloomsbury Publishing, 2012.

Xenophon, *Hellenica*, ed. G. Cawkwell, Penguin, 1979.

Map of Attica

Plan of Athens

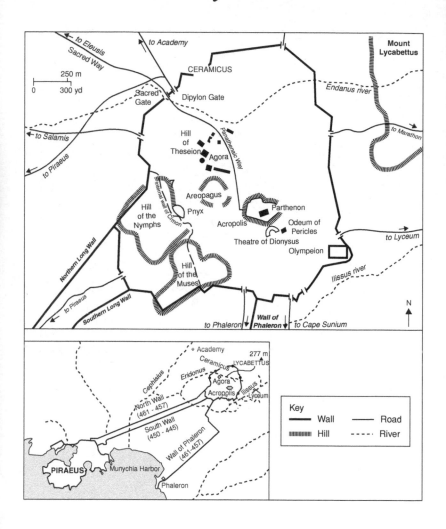

List of characters

DIONYSUS

XANTHIAS

HERACLES

CORPSE

CHARON

CHORUS OF FROGS

CHORUS OF INITIATES

AEACUS

MAID

INNKEEPER 1 (Pandoceutria)

INNKEEPER 2 (Plathane)

SLAVE OF PLUTO

EURIPIDES

AESCHYLUS

PLUTO

PROLOGUE (1–315): comic warm-up

Aristophanes opens with what feels more like a well-worn stand-up comedy routine than a play. Even to a modern audience this double act feels instantly familiar. We learn that the slave's name is Xanthias at 271; his superior master identifies himself as a god at 22.

Types of humour

Various types of humour are on display here, from the visual slapstick of an overloaded slave riding a donkey, to verbal wit and banter as the two argue about who's doing the work. There is innuendo and scatological humour involving bodily functions (**dump**, 9; **fart**, 10; **puke**, 12), and some feeble jokes that Dionysus crushes before Xanthias can come out with them (2–9).

○ Act this scene out in front of an audience. At which moments, if any, do they laugh? How could a pair of actors make the most of this opening?

○ How might costumes (see 47–8) or sound effects help?

○ Is the absence of stage directions in the text (see **'Stage direction'**, p. 24) liberating or unhelpful?

14–15 Phrynichus ... Lycis and Ameipsias The only complete comedies to survive from this period are by Aristophanes, but other great playwrights are known from fragments of their works and other sources. **Phrynichus** (son of Eunomides) was in direct competition with Aristophanes at the Lenaea of 405 BC where his play, *The Muses*, came second after *Frogs*. **Ameipsias** was another successful comic poet who competed against Aristophanes in the late fifth century. Little is known of **Lycis** and no fragment of his plays survives.

21 the limit The Greek is *hubris*. Xanthias, a cheeky slave, oversteps the mark, provoking his master and a god, but this is a comedy, without the consequences of tragic *hubris*.

22 I, Dionysus, son of Flagon It was not unusual for gods to appear on the Athenian stage. For example, Euripides' *Bacchae* (see 67n) opens with the announcement *I Dionysus, son of Zeus, have come to this land of Thebes*. Dionysus' claim here to be the son of a flagon highlights his role as god of wine, but Dionysus was also god of the theatre. The plays at the Lenaea and City Dionysia were performed in his sanctuary, at his festivals.

XANTHIAS Should I tell one of the usual, sir? One the audience
always laughs at?

DIONYSUS Fine, whatever you want – but not, 'I'm feeling the
pressure.' Keep off that one. It's so irritating.

XANTHIAS Some other little witticism, then?   5

DIONYSUS Yes, anything except 'I am really feeling the squeeze.'

XANTHIAS Oh. Shall I tell them a really funny one?

DIONYSUS For god's sake, out with it. Only don't …

XANTHIAS Don't what?

DIONYSUS … shift your pole around and say you need a dump.

XANTHIAS I've such a load that if I can't relieve myself, I'll fart it all   10
away …

DIONYSUS No, please. Wait until I really need to puke.

XANTHIAS Then why do I have to carry all this equipment, if I
don't get to do any of that stuff you see in Phrynichus' plays?
Lycis and Ameipsias always have baggage-handling routines in   15
their comedies.

DIONYSUS Just don't. Whenever I go to the theatre and see one of
those jokes, I come away with a year off my life.

XANTHIAS O thrice ill-fated shoulders! My neck's so squished it   20
can't even tell a joke.

DIONYSUS This is the limit. It's what comes of spoiling him. Here
am I, Dionysus, son of Flagon, and I am the one walking and
doing all the hard work. I let him ride so that he won't get worn
out by carrying the burden.

XANTHIAS And aren't I the one carrying it?   25

DIONYSUS How can you be carrying it, when you are the burden?

XANTHIAS I'm carrying all this.

DIONYSUS And how are you bearing it?

XANTHIAS Very badly.

DIONYSUS Now this burden you're bearing – isn't the donkey
carrying it?

XANTHIAS Definitely not. I've got it, I'm the one bearing it – not
the donkey, goddammit.

DIONYSUS But how can you be doing the carrying, when you are
actually being carried by something else?

XANTHIAS I don't know. But my shoulder's feeling the pressure.   30

34 that sea-battle! The sea-battle of Arginusae was in 406 BC (*Background to the story*, pp. v–vii; Xenophon, *Hellenica* 1.6.24). The Athenians had rebuilt their navy under great pressure after defeats at Notium and Mytilene earlier in the year. Recruitment now extended to slaves, who earned their freedom (see 694n). Many slaves had already gone over to the enemy, conveniently based at Decelea in Attica, but this policy limited further defections.

Heracles (see also illustration, p. 8)

The door is opened by a character instantly recognisable to the audience as Heracles (the Greek name for Hercules). Over his own traditional **yellow** gown (48), a colour worn by women, Dionysus is dressed in *his* costume: the skin of the Nemean lion and the club he used to defeat it. Rather than looking heroic in this outfit, Dionysus appears ridiculous. Dionysus mistakes Heracles' amusement for fear.

38 like a centaur These half-man, half-horse creatures were renowned for their rough, uncivilised ways, especially when drunk.

44–5 By Demeter The dialogue is littered with oaths, even by gods. **By Zeus** appears about fifty times in the Greek text of *Frogs*. Demeter, Apollo and Poseidon are also regularly invoked.

48 Cleisthenes Mentioned in almost all of Aristophanes' plays, he is routinely mocked for his passive homosexuality (see 57, 422). Wealthy Athenians, such as Cleisthenes, might be liable for a special form of taxation which involved sponsoring a play or equipping a trireme.

50–1 twelve or thirteen enemy ships Towards the end of the war, the Spartan fleet regularly numbered over a hundred ships. Dionysus' boast would constitute a major victory for a fleet, never mind an individual ship or two crew members.

53 reading *Andromeda* The Athenians generally encountered tragedy only in performance at the dramatic festivals, but here is evidence that written texts were available (see 943n, 1115, 1410).

55 Just a little one – the size of Molon Comic irony may be confusing: ancient commentators suggest that Molon was a large actor.

56 for a boy? Although Dionysus is taken aback at the suggestion, paedophilia was a feature of Athenian life, idealised in art. The suggestion that Dionysus' passion is **For a man** is more insulting.

DIONYSUS Since you say the donkey's no help to you, swap over.
You pick the donkey up and carry him instead.

XANTHIAS Ah woe is me, poor wretch! Why didn't I fight in that
sea-battle! Then I could tell you to bugger off.

DIONYSUS Get down, you idiot. My journey's taken me right up to   35
this door here, my first destination.
Slave, I say, slave, slave!

HERACLES Who's that battering the door, flinging himself at it like
a centaur? Who the … say, what is all this?

DIONYSUS Slave.

XANTHIAS What is it?   40

DIONYSUS Did you notice that?

XANTHIAS Notice what exactly?

DIONYSUS How scared he was of me.

XANTHIAS Oh, yes, by Zeus – scared that you're a maniac.

HERACLES By Demeter, I just can't stop laughing. I'm biting my lip,
but I just can't stop myself.   45

DIONYSUS My good chap, step forward. I have a favour to ask of
you.

HERACLES I can't stop laughing – look at that lionskin on top of
your little yellow number. What's the idea? Why these boots and
club? Where on earth were you heading?

DIONYSUS I was sailing with Cleisthenes.

HERACLES You fought at sea?

DIONYSUS Yes, and sank – oh, must have been twelve or thirteen   50
enemy ships.

HERACLES The two of you?

DIONYSUS Yes, by Apollo.

XANTHIAS In your dreams …

DIONYSUS And while I was on board, reading *Andromeda* to
myself, a sudden desire filled my heart – you wouldn't believe
how strong it was.

HERACLES Desire? What kind of desire?   55

DIONYSUS Just a little one – the size of Molon.

HERACLES For a woman?

DIONYSUS No, no, no!

HERACLES Then for a boy?

58–60 my brother ... little brother Both Dionysus and Heracles were sons of Zeus. Alcmene bore Heracles, Semele conceived Dionysus.

Euripides (66)

Euripides is one of three great Greek tragedians, along with Aeschylus and Sophocles, whose work was deliberately preserved in antiquity. Although Euripides was the least successful of the three in terms of poetic prizes (he won five first prizes at the City Dionysia, compared to Aeschylus' 13 and Sophocles' 18), more of his plays (19) have survived complete. He was a well-known figure in Athens, caricatured by Aristophanes in *Thesmophoriazusae*, 411 BC. Euripides' lost tragedy *Andromeda* (53) is parodied in the same play.

Plot

So far the audience have been left to guess the nature of the plot. Our first clue comes with the mention of Euripides. More will be revealed.

67 Even though he's dead? A necrophiliac joke completes Heracles' attempts to find out what excites Dionysus. An ancient anecdote tells of news of Euripides' death in Macedon reaching Athens in time for Sophocles to show his respect: chorus and actors appeared without the customary crowns in the procession before Sophocles' final production in the City Dionysia of 406 BC. Sophocles died in that year, perhaps too late for Aristophanes to make more than a few gracious references in *Frogs* (82, 787–9, 1515–19). Euripides' final victory at the City Dionysia was posthumously awarded a few months after *Frogs*, for a trilogy including *Bacchae*, still one of his most popular plays.

74 Iophon Sophocles' son won first prize in 435 BC and came second to Euripides in 428 BC; 50 plays (all lost) have been attributed to him. He may not be quite as reliant on his father as Dionysus implies.

83 Agathon The setting of Plato's *Symposium* is a dinner party celebrating Agathon's first triumph at the Lenaea of 416 BC, with his dazzling speech praising love; he also appears in Aristophanes' *Thesmophoriazusae*, caricatured as a talented but temperamental transvestite. Agathon's plays were much admired, but few fragments survive. At 86, **banquet of the blest** is less a euphemism for death than a hint at the comforts of the court of King Archelaus in Macedon, where Agathon and Euripides both chose to retire from Athenian life.

86–7 Xenocles ... Pythangelos? Like Iophon, **Xenocles** followed in his father's steps and wrote tragedies. He is caricatured as a little crab (a play on Carcinus, his father's name) in Aristophanes' *Wasps* and parodied in *Clouds*, 1266. **Pythangelos** is otherwise unknown.

DIONYSUS Certainly not.

HERACLES For a man?

DIONYSUS Argh!

HERACLES Well, you were with Cleisthenes.

DIONYSUS Don't make fun of me, my brother. I really am in a bad
way. The longing's so strong it'll kill me.

HERACLES What kind of longing, little brother?   60

DIONYSUS I can't explain. Let me try an analogy: have you ever felt
a sudden craving for lentil soup?

HERACLES Lentil soup? Mmm-mmm. Thousands of times in my
life.

DIONYSUS Am I explaining clearly, or should I put it in another
way?

HERACLES No, no. Lentil soup. I understand perfectly about lentils.   65

DIONYSUS Well, just such a craving consumes me – for Euripides.

HERACLES Even though he's dead?

DIONYSUS No mortal alive could keep me from going after him.

HERACLES Then you would descend to the underworld?

DIONYSUS Yes, by Zeus, and the under-underworld, if there is one.   70

HERACLES What do you want?

DIONYSUS I need a good poet. Those that aren't dead are dread-ful.

HERACLES What? Isn't Iophon still around?

DIONYSUS He is the only good thing left, if he is any good.
Actually, I don't even know that.   75

HERACLES Then why don't you fetch Sophocles rather than
Euripides, if you must bring someone back?

DIONYSUS Not until I have got Iophon on his own, without
Sophocles, to test what he's made of. Anyway, Euripides is a
complete crook and would have a go at running away from the   80
underworld with me, whereas Sophocles is completely
easy-going, wherever he is.

HERACLES And where's Agathon?

DIONYSUS Gone and left us. A good poet, a good friend, much
missed.

HERACLES Where on earth did the poor fellow end up?   85

DIONYSUS The banquet of the blest.

HERACLES And Xenocles?

87 No mention of me While Xanthias can't expect a mention as an up-and-coming tragedian, he would like to be noticed. His whines to the audience, upstaging the action, become a running joke (107, 115).

95 a tragic chorus Three dramatists were selected to compete several months before the festival by a senior magistrate or *archōn*. A wealthy citizen – the *chorēgos* – was appointed to finance the chorus and other aspects of production, a tax comparable to financing a trireme (see 48n).

98 What do you mean, original? Dionysus recites Euripidean lines: **foot of time** (100) is in *Bacchae* 889; the last phrase is a garbled version of *Hippolytus* 612, *it was my tongue that swore, not my heart*, a notoriously slippery and sophistic defence of perjury (see **'Review of the character of Euripides'**, p. 100).

107 Stick to what you know Dionysus warns Heracles off his territory. As god of theatre, judging poetry is his domain, whereas Heracles was a notorious glutton. In a democracy, though, everyone was a critic and a modern audience may sympathise with Heracles.

Heracles' twelfth labour

Caeretan black-figure hydria, 6th century BC, Musée du Louvre. Heracles abducting Cerberus from Hades' house, the last of 12 labours imposed on him by King Eurystheus (see 466n). He wears the skin of the Nemean lion and carries his club.

Plan

Dionysus now reveals the full purpose of his visit. He needs to go down to the underworld to retrieve Euripides and has come to ask for some travel tips, since Heracles made the journey himself when completing his final labour. As we shall see, Heracles' visit has not been forgotten by others in the underworld (see 464–588).

Problem

Since Dionysus seems to be in a hurry, Heracles gives tips on sudden death: hanging, poisoning and leaping off a tall building. Dionysus objects, not on the grounds that he's immortal (and therefore can't die) but because these methods sound unpleasant.

DIONYSUS Dead, for all I care.

HERACLES Pythangelos?

XANTHIAS No mention of me, with my shoulder completely worn
away.

HERACLES Aren't there lots of other chappies writing tragedies up
here – thousands of them – churning out far more than   90
Euripides?

DIONYSUS Slim pickings. A flock of artistic tits twittering away. A
disgrace to their profession. Once they've got their hands on a
tragic chorus, they piss on the opportunity and vanish. Gone.   95
Even if you looked, you couldn't find an original poet able to
construct a noble phrase.

HERACLES What do you mean, original?

DIONYSUS I mean someone adventurous, someone who'll risk a
phrase like *the airy apartment of Zeus* or *the foot of time*, or *a*   100
mind that refuses to swear on oath, but a tongue that's sworn
already, never mind the mind.

HERACLES You like that stuff?

DIONYSUS Actually, I'm crrrazy for it.

HERACLES It's a load of cobblers – you must see that.

DIONYSUS Get out of my brain. Stay in your own.   105

HERACLES But it's obviously complete and utter rubbish.

DIONYSUS Stick to what you know – food!

XANTHIAS No mention of me!

DIONYSUS No. The reason I came here dressed like you was so that
you could give me your contacts, the ones you used that time   110
you went after Cerberus. Just in case I need them. I want the
following: the ports, the bakeries, the porn-shops, the rest-areas,
where to turn off and get a drink, the streets, the cities, the
rooms to rent, what the landladies are like and where you won't
find too many bed-bugs.

XANTHIAS No mention of me!   115

HERACLES You crazy fool, do *you* dare go as well?

DIONYSUS One last question, then. What is the quickest route to
the underworld? Nothing too hot or cold.

HERACLES Hmm, which shall I mention first? Let's see. There is   120

124 hemlock This plant could be ground to create a poison. An account of its use by the state to execute criminals is found in Plato's idealised description of Socrates' death (*Phaedo* 117e–18).

128 Ceramicus The potters' quarter in Athens (our word 'ceramic' comes from it) extending from the agora to and beyond the Dipylon gate. Appropriately, it incorporated part of the cemetery outside the walls. The **tall tower** (130) has not been identified, but this was the route taken by runners in ritual torch-races (132) held at night (see plan of Athens, p. x).

Homer's underworld

In Homer's *Odyssey* 10.508–14 (see also Odyssey 11 and 24, and *Iliad* 23.71–3), Circe directs Odysseus to the underworld: *But when you pass through Ocean in your ship, there lies a fertile shore and Persephone's grove with tall poplars and seed-shedding willows. Beach your boat… and go yourself to Hades' dank house, where Fire-blazing Phlegython, and Cocytus, River of Screams, tributary of Styx, flow into Acheron.*

Death in Homer is bleak and frightening: unburied souls flit squeaking like bats; even those that are buried, who can *pass through Hades' gates* and *mingle with those beyond the river* are frail and bloodless. Homer mentions Cerberus briefly (see 466n) but not Charon (see p. 14 and illustration p. 16). Minos judges the dead and some (e.g. Tantalus, 1232n) are condemned, but the moral judgement of minor crooks is more characteristic of Orphic (1032–5n) than Homeric death, where heroes stride indiscriminately across asphodel meadows.

● What similarities to and differences from the Homeric world of the dead are there in Heracles' description (137–64)?

Eleusinian Mysteries

The *Homeric Hymn to Demeter* offers an alternative to Homer's bleak picture of death for those initiated into the goddess's Mysteries. A significant number of Athenians were initiated into annual rites celebrating the idea of rebirth and hope for the afterlife, based on the story of Demeter and Persephone (see 336n and **'Demeter'**, p. 28). The ceremonies at the climax are not revealed by ancient sources, but remains of the sanctuary survive. Details of the initial sacrifices and the 22 km procession of initiates from Athens to Eleusis are known.

140 two obols The usual fee for the ferryman was one obol (173n), placed in the mouth of the dead. The term *diobelea* (two obols) had recently become widespread in Athens after a measure introduced by Cleophon (see 1504n) in 410 BC, which offered income relief to the poor. **Theseus** was the only Athenian known to have entered Hades.

one way by rope and stool – involves a bit of hanging around.

DIONYSUS Stop. That must be some kind of choke.

HERACLES Then there's the direct route – chop, chop – via pestle and mortar.

DIONYSUS You mean – hemlock?

HERACLES Absolutely.   125

DIONYSUS A cold, wintry way. Your extrrremities get frrrozen rrright off.

HERACLES Want me to tell you a quick, downhill route?

DIONYSUS Yes, because I'm no walk-aholic.

HERACLES Tip-toe down to the Ceramicus…

DIONYSUS And then?

HERACLES Climb up that tall tower…   130

DIONYSUS Then what?

HERACLES From up at the top, watch the start of the torch-race, and then, when the spectators say 'Go!' you go too.

DIONYSUS Where?

HERACLES Down.

DIONYSUS But that would make mincemeat of my medulla. I don't   135
like that way.

HERACLES So which way, then?

DIONYSUS The way you took when you went down.

HERACLES The journey's gi-normous. You'll come straightaway to a marsh; it's huge and completely bottomless.

DIONYSUS Then how do I get to the other side?

HERACLES In a tiny little boat – an old man, a sailor, will take you across, once he's paid. It costs two obols.   140

DIONYSUS Wow. The universal power of two obols!
How did they get down there?

HERACLES Theseus introduced them.
After this, you'll see snakes and wild animals, thousands of them, really terrible…

DIONYSUS Don't try to scare or frighten me. You won't succeed.   145

HERACLES …and then a lot of mud and free-flowing shit. And lying in this you'll see anyone who ever at any time wronged a

152 Morsimus The last crime in this shocking list provides a comic anticlimax. The tragedian Morsimus is treated with contempt elsewhere by Aristophanes (*Knights* 401, *Peace* 802).

153 Cinesias (see 366n, Round 5 p. 98) His airy dithyrambic songs to Dionysus are parodied by other comedians as well as by Aristophanes in *Birds* (1372ff) and *Gerytades*, a lost play. The **war-dance** (153) was a competitive event, included in the four-yearly Great Panathenaic festival (see '**Torch-race**', p. 74).

162 Pluto Hades is also known as Pluto. The Greek word *ploutos* means wealthy. Hades' realm grows richer each day with the dead.

Apulian red-figure volute krater; Underworld Painter, 330–320 BC. Includes: Hades and Persephone (centre); Orpheus (left); three judges: Rhadamanthus, Minos and Aeacus (right); Hercules and Cerberus (below). Munich, Antikensammlung.

Burial of the dead

Many depictions of Athenian funerals survive from this period. The dead are laid out (*prothesis*), then carried in procession (*ekphora*) on a bier, sometimes on wheels, for cremation or burial, perhaps marked with a grave *stēlē* or in a sarcophagus. Male and female mourners usually attend. The corpse in this passage is accompanied, it seems, only by his bearers, whom he addresses imperiously in line 174.

173 two drachmas Charon charged 2 obols. A skilled craftsman might earn 1 drachma a day, worth 6 obols, so this is expensive.

guest, or nicked the pocket-money of a boy while bonking him, or beat up his mother or whacked his father on the jaw, or swore 150 a false oath or copied down a monologue from Morsimus.

DIONYSUS God, yes – and let's add to the list anyone who's learnt that war-dance of Cinesias.

HERACLES Next the breath of pipes will float around you, and you will see a pure, beautiful light, like you get up here; and myrtle 155 groves and happy bands of men and women and lots of hand-clapping.

DIONYSUS Who are they, then?

HERACLES The Initiates of the Mysteries.

XANTHIAS By the gods, the only mystery is why I am such an ass, carrying all this. I won't hold on to it any more. 160

HERACLES They will tell you everything you need. They live right next to the road that goes straight to the gates of Pluto. And so, a very good goodbye, my brother.

DIONYSUS And to you too, by Zeus. Keep well. 165
You, pick up the baggage again.

XANTHIAS Before I've even put it down?

DIONYSUS Absolutely. And quick about it.

XANTHIAS No, I beg you. Please hire one of the corpses they're taking for burial. They're going our way.

DIONYSUS And if I can't find one?

XANTHIAS Then I'll have to do.

DIONYSUS Good idea. And here's a corpse they're bringing now. 170
Hey you! Yes you, the stiff. Do you want to carry this luggage to the underworld?

CORPSE How many pieces?

DIONYSUS Just these.

CORPSE It'll cost two drachmas.

DIONYSUS God, too much.

CORPSE You lot, carry on!

DIONYSUS Wait, my good chap. Maybe we can come to an 175 arrangement.

CORPSE If you can't pay two drachmas, we have nothing to discuss.

DIONYSUS Here are nine obols.

178 Strike me alive Aristophanes has fun with the humorous possibilities suggested by this scene, from the dramatic irony of the bier appearing on cue and the incongruity of a corpse haggling about money (or being sorry, 178) to puns and jokes about death.

● What would be lost if this short scene (167–79) were cut?

Charon (see illustration, p. 16)

Charon is not mentioned in the Homeric underworld, but he was a familiar figure in Athenian art by the mid 5th century. A Greek writer who visited Egypt in the 1st century BC suggests Egyptian origins, recording local funerary customs as follows:

When the body is ready to be buried the family affirms that he who has just passed away 'is about to cross the lake'. Then ... the boat is launched, in the charge of the boatman whom the Egyptians in their language name Charon. Diodorus Siculus 1.91ff (see also 1032–5n)

184 XAIPE XAPΩN (khaire, kharon) Dionysus greets the ferryman using the Greek for hello/goodbye (**CHAIRE**), a pun on Charon's name. **Ō-op, op** (181, 209) gives an impression of the sound of his rowing.

186 Forgetfulness Forgetfulness is Lethe, a river in the underworld. **Lethargy** (*Ocnus* in Greek) is an allegorical figure in a lost painting of the underworld by the famous 5th-century painter Polygnotus:

A seated man is depicted plaiting a rope. A she-mule stands beside him constantly munching away at the rope he has woven. They say that this man Ocnus used to love his work, but he had an extravagant wife, and everything he earned, she quickly spent. Pausanias 10.29.1

187 go to hell or Damnation Literally translated, this is 'go to the crows or Taenarum'. The former is a common curse; the latter was believed to be an entrance to the underworld at the tip of the Peloponnese.

192 a bit of an eye infection Xanthias probably shows more resourcefulness than honesty in explaining why he didn't join up to fight at Arginusae. Cure records from the sanctuary of Asclepius at Epidaurus show eye disease to be the most commonly attested ailment.

Rowing class

The Athenian audience knew a thing or two about rowing as a result of their naval supremacy. Athenian class was dictated largely by military considerations: the wealthiest citizens were in the cavalry (*hippeis*). In Aristophanes' *Knights* they make up the long-haired, foppish chorus. Those who could afford their own personal armour made up the *hoplite* class. The remainder (*thētes*) joined the all-important fleet (with the addition of slaves in 406 BC). The humour here comes from Dionysus' aristocratic ignorance: unlike most of his audience, he has no idea what to do with an oar – and is about to discover the discomforts of rowing.

CORPSE Nine obols! Strike me alive if ...

XANTHIAS Sanctimonious little bastard. He'll be sorry ...
I'll just carry on, then.

DIONYSUS You are an honest, decent chap. Let's board the boat. 180

CHARON *Ô-op.* Bring her alongside.

XANTHIAS What is this?

DIONYSUS This? It's a marsh, by Zeus, the one he told us about.
And I see a boat.

XANTHIAS Holy Poseidon, that must be Charon.

DIONYSUS Calling Charon. Come in, Charon. ΧΑΙΡΕ, ΧΑΡΩΝ!!!!!

CHARON Anyone for Strife-end, Troubles-ease or the Plains of 185
Forgetfulness? The Rope of Lethargy? Outer Cerberia?
Who wants to go to hell or Damnation?

DIONYSUS Oh, yes, me!

CHARON Get on quickly.

DIONYSUS Where are you going?

CHARON To hell.

DIONYSUS Really?

CHARON Yes, by Zeus. At your service. Get in, then. 190

DIONYSUS Slave, come here.

CHARON I don't carry slaves. Not if they didn't fight for their lives
in that sea-battle.

XANTHIAS Not me, I'm afraid. I happened to have a bit of an eye
infection at the time.

CHARON So you'll be running round the marsh, then?

XANTHIAS Yes. Where will I wait for you?

CHARON By Withering Heights, at the ferry-stop. 195

DIONYSUS Do you understand?

XANTHIAS All too well. Poor me, what did I do this morning to
deserve this?

CHARON Sit at your oar. Anyone else for the crossing, hurry up.
Hey you, what are you doing?

DIONYSUS What am I doing? Just sitting by the oar, like you told
me.

CHARON Your seat's here, fatty. 200

DIONYSUS Right.

CHARON Put your hands forward and pull.

205 Salamis (see map, p. ix) An island off Attica and the site of the proudest naval victory for the Athenians, the defeat of the great Persian fleet in 480 BC (Herodotus, *Histories* 8.78–96).

Chorus

Charon's introduction to the musical **swan-frogs** (207) prepares us for music and singing from the chorus which gives the play its name.

This should be the spectacular moment everyone's been waiting for, when the Chorus, magnificently costumed and trained at great expense (see 95n), arrive on stage and stay for the rest of the play. In fact, it's a false lead – the real Chorus don't arrive until line 316 (**'Parodos'**, p. 24). Perhaps the frogs were heard but not seen in the original performance. Modern productions with fewer restrictions have made the most of this moment (see illustration, p. 18).

216 Nysian Zeus bore Dionysus from his thigh on Mount Nysa.

Charon ferries the souls of the dead. Sabouroff Painter, mid 5th century. National Museum, Athens.

217 On the Day of Pots The Anthesteria or Festival of Flowers was an Athenian drinking festival to Dionysus held directly after the Lenaea in February. The third day of drinking was called the Chutroi, or Day of Pots. It was one of the older festivals, held in the sanctuary of Dionysus in the marshes, south of the agora (Thucydides, *History of the Peloponnesian War* 2.16.4).

Greek frogs

The sound of Aristophanes' frogs, *bre-ke-ke-kex, co-ax, co-ax*, can still be heard in Greece – e.g. at Olympia, and in marshes, Stygian or otherwise. Frogs are also found in Greek literature, in Aesop's fables and the mock epic *Batrachomyomachia* (*Battle of Frogs and Mice*).

DIONYSUS Right-o.

CHARON Stop being an idiot. Take the strain and row. Hard.

DIONYSUS How can I? I've never tried, never been at sea, never been near Salamis. How can I row?

CHARON It's very easy. Once you've dipped your oar in for the first time, you'll hear the sweetest melodies.

DIONYSUS What kind of melodies?

CHARON The amazing melodies of swan-frogs.

DIONYSUS Right-o. Give the order.

CHARON *Ō-op, op. Ō-op, op.*

CHORUS OF FROGS   *Bre-ke-ke-kex, co-ax, co-ax,*
                              Bre-ke-ke-kex, co-ax, co-ax.
                              Marshy children of the lake,
                              Let's sing out our harmonies,
                              Uttering sweet melodies
                              In tuneful song,
                                   Co-ax, co-ax.
                              A song for Dionysus,
                              Nysian son of Zeus,
                              Will be our Bacchic cry
                              When revellers
                              On the Day of Pots
                              Pass drunken
                              Through my sanctuary,
                              A merry mob.
                              Bre-ke-ke-kex, co-ax, co-ax.

DIONYSUS   I am beginning to feel a pain
                              – in the arse.
                              Co-ax, co-ax.

CHORUS OF FROGS *Bre-ke-ke-kex, co-ax, co-ax.*

DIONYSUS But you probably don't care.

CHORUS OF FROGS   *Bre-ke-ke-kex, co-ax, co-ax.*

DIONYSUS   To hell with your *co-ax*,
                              You're nothing but *co-ax*.

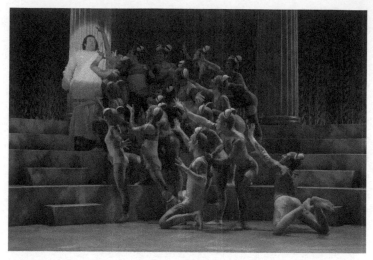

Frogs *(adapted by Stephen Sondheim and Burt Shelove), Point Park Conservatory Theater, Pittsburgh, 2007; directed by Scott Wise. Thomas Sullivan as Heracles and Dale Spollett as Dionysus.*

249 froggle-bubble-splash-dash Aristophanes likes inventing words. In Greek this is *pompholygopaphlasmasin* (literally 'bubble-gush-splutter', representing the noise of bubbles rising in water).

Dionysus
This is the first of the poetic contests in the play – an unedifying shouting match between the god of drama and some marsh-frogs. In Greek they use lyric rhythmical patterns which would have been sung.

● Who wins and how?
● What impressions of Dionysus have you formed from the play so far? Which of the following adjectives best suit him?
divine, masterful, cowardly, dignified, ridiculous, boastful, self-centred, witty, feeble

CHORUS OF FROGS Mind your own business.

What did you expect?

I'm loved by the Muses, with their beautiful lyres,

And by horn-footed Pan who plays on his pipe. 230

Tuneful Apollo likes me, too:

For the watery reeds,

Which I grow in the marshes,

Make bridges for his lyre.

Bre-ke-ke-kex, co-ax, co-ax. 235

DIONYSUS But I've got blisters.

My bum is wet

And just about to poo.

Something will pop out and say…

CHORUS OF FROGS *Bre-ke-ke-kex, co-ax, co-ax.*

DIONYSUS Song-loving race, please stop! 240

CHORUS OF FROGS Oh no, we'll sing all the more,

If ever in days of glorious sun

We've jumped through the marsh grass

And flowering rush,

Taking delight in the leaping

Strains of our song; 245

Or away from the raindrops sent by Zeus

We've sung and danced

In the glimmering depths

With a froggle-bubble-splash-dash.

DIONYSUS+FROGS *Bre-ke-ke-kex, co-ax, co-ax.* 250

DIONYSUS I'm borrowing your refrain.

FROGS That will cause us horrible pain.

DIONYSUS Not as much as I will hurt

If this rowing makes me pop! 255

DIONYSUS+FROGS *Bre-ke-ke-kex, co-ax, co-ax.*

DIONYSUS Wail away – see if I care.

CHORUS OF FROGS Indeed, we will croak

All day,

As long as our throats can take it. 260

DIONYSUS+FROGS *Bre-ke-ke-kex, co-ax, co-ax.*

Reunion

Xanthias' adventures are not reported. He was probably not allowed on the boat for practical as well as snobbish reasons (193–4). Space might be tight, especially if staging the rowing scene involved use of the *ekkyklēma*, a platform that could be wheeled out of the *skēnē*.

275–277 father-killers and oath-breakers ... I can still see them now This is probably a moment of audience involvement as Dionysus studies the crowd (see also 297).

278 this is the place where ... Heracles' directions at 136–64 have already proved useful. His advice gives structure to the first half of this play in the same way that Circe's directions to Odysseus (see p. 10) give shape to Books 11 and 12 of the *Odyssey*.

Comic business

The reunited duo perform another classic comedy routine.

- Which modern comedy duo could you most easily imagine performing this scene (272–315)?

Scooby Doo and Shaggy.

DIONYSUS	You won't win at this.
CHORUS OF FROGS	You're not going to beat us – no way!
DIONYSUS	And you'll never beat me.

Not ever! For I will *co-ax*
All day, if I must.   265
'Til I get the better of your
Co-ax.
BRE-KE-KE-KEX, CO-AX, CO-AX.

There. I knew I'd stop that *co-ax* in the end.

CHARON Stop, stop. Bring her alongside with the oars.
Give me the fare and get out.   270

DIONYSUS Here you are, two obols.

Xanthias! Where are you, Xanthias? Hey, Xanthias!

XANTHIAS Ho, there!

DIONYSUS Come here.

XANTHIAS Hello, master.

DIONYSUS What's that over there?

XANTHIAS Darkness and filth.

DIONYSUS I suppose you saw the father-killers and oath-breakers   275
he told us about.

XANTHIAS Didn't you?

DIONYSUS Oh, yes, by Poseidon, I certainly did, and I can still see
them now. OK, what do we do next?

XANTHIAS We'd best keep moving, because this is the place where
Heracles said the wild beasts were.

DIONYSUS He'll be sorry. He was just bragging to make me afraid,   280
knowing what a good fighter I am. Pure envy. He's so conceited.
But I'm praying that I *do* meet something and carry off a trophy
worthy of the trip.

XANTHIAS By Zeus, I can hear a noise.   285

DIONYSUS Where? Where is it?

XANTHIAS Behind.

DIONYSUS Get behind me. Now!

XANTHIAS But it's in front.

DIONYSUS Quick. Get in front.

293 Empusa Xanthias describes a terrifying, mysterious and ridiculous shape-shifting bogey-woman, whom Dionysus calls Empusa. Empusa is associated with Hecate (1363n) who played a role in the Eleusinian Mysteries.

298 Priest Roman copies of the special seats preserved for officials may still be seen in the theatre of Dionysus at Athens. The priest of Dionysus sat in the centre of the front row. As in line 277, the actors interact with the audience, 'breaking the fourth wall', the imaginary line in traditional Western theatre that separates the audience from the drama. Dionysus' offer in Greek translates more literally, 'I'll be your fellow drinker.'

305 *weasel* Xanthias reminds the audience of a classic mispronunciation by the actor Hegelochus playing the part of Orestes three years earlier. In Greek the words **calm** and **weasel** are similar. In translation, it's supposed to be a mispronounced 'calm we'll see'.

308 tunic; turned brown For Dionysus' incontinence (see 479).

311 Xanthias throws back Dionysus' favourite phrases from line 100.

XANTHIAS Oh, my god, I can see a huge beast.

DIONYSUS What's it like?

XANTHIAS Terrible. It takes any form – one moment it's a bull, next   290
it's a wildass, then it's a woman – absolutely gorgeous!

DIONYSUS Where? Here, let me go to her …

XANTHIAS But she's not a woman any more. She's a dog.

DIONYSUS It must be Empusa.

XANTHIAS Her whole face is blazing with light.

DIONYSUS And does she have a bronze leg?

XANTHIAS Oh, yes, by Poseidon. And the other one's made of   295
cow-poo – as you can tell.

DIONYSUS Where should I turn?

XANTHIAS Or I?

DIONYSUS Priest, save me – I'll get you a drink after the show.

XANTHIAS Lord Heracles, we're dead!

DIONYSUS Please, my dear chap. Don't expect me to do anything.
And don't use that name.

XANTHIAS Dionysus, then.   300

DIONYSUS That's even worse!

XANTHIAS Then keep going.
Here, over here, master!

DIONYSUS What is it?

XANTHIAS You can cheer up now. We've done just fine. Hegelochus
was right. We can say, *After the storm, a calm weasel.* Empusa has   305
gone.

DIONYSUS Swear it!

XANTHIAS I swear it by Zeus.

DIONYSUS Swear it again.

XANTHIAS By Zeus.

DIONYSUS Swear.

XANTHIAS By Zeus.

DIONYSUS Alas, poor me! How pale I was when I saw her.

XANTHIAS I am afraid your tunic's turned brown from fright.

DIONYSUS Oh no! Whence came this dreadful calamity?
Which god should I blame for my undoing?   310

XANTHIAS *The airy apartment of Zeus* or *the foot of time*?

DIONYSUS Hey!

314 most mysterious Pine torches and flute music were both associated with religious festivals. The word **mysterious** hints at what's to come. Dionysus and Xanthias are about to eavesdrop on the **Initiates of the Mysteries** (318), as Heracles had advised (158).

PARODOS (316–459)

The arrival of the chorus was highly anticipated in any Athenian tragedy or comedy: 24 young Athenian men costumed and trained at the expense of the *chorēgos* (see 95n) entered the *orchēstra* singing and dancing. Most choruses are all male (e.g. old Thebans in *Antigone*) or all female (e.g. in Euripides' *Bacchae* and Aristophanes' *Clouds*). These **Initiates of the Mysteries** (see p. 10 and pp. 154–8) include males and females (409–12). They change the atmosphere completely and may have brought a touch of nostalgia; while the Spartans occupied Decelea in 413 BC, the annual Eleusinian procession in September had to be suspended, although Alcibiades (see *Background to the story*, pp. v–vii; **'Parodying the Mysteries'**, p. 32; **Round 5**, p. 96) flamboyantly reinstated the tradition for 407 BC (Plutarch, *Alcibiades* 34).

Stage direction

The text has a stage direction between lines 315 and 316; these are not generally included. For **pipes** see **'Lyric passages'**, p. 86.

316 Iacchus The name of this youthful Eleusinian god who led the Initiates carrying a torch is derived from the joyous cry *iacchē*. His image was carried from Athens to Eleusis in the procession. Dionysus or Bacchus is sometimes also called by this name (e.g. *Bacchae* 725).

A woman with a basket sacrifices a pig. The three torches represent the underworld. Athens New Museum; lekythos, c. 450 BC. Pigs, sacred to Demeter, were sacrificed during the Eleusinian Mysteries.

XANTHIAS What is it?

DIONYSUS Did you hear that?

XANTHIAS Hear what?

DIONYSUS The sound of pipes.

XANTHIAS I certainly did. And a most mysterious wafting of pine
torches has come over me.

DIONYSUS Let's crouch down here quietly and have a listen.   315

[Someone plays the pipes inside]

CHORUS OF INITIATES   Iacchus, Iacchus!
                             Iacchus, Iacchus!

XANTHIAS That's it, master. It's those Initiates prancing around.
The ones Heracles told us about. They're singing that song to
Iacchus you hear everywhere.   320

DIONYSUS I think you're right.
Best keep quiet, then, so we know for sure.

CHORUS OF INITIATES   Iacchus, honoured god,
                Whose home and resting place is here!
                             Iacchus! Iacchus!   325
                    Come into this meadow to dance
                        And join your sacred band,
                      Shaking the garland of myrtle,
                       Bursting with ripe berries,
                          That crowns your head,   330
                        Drumming with bold feet
                        Your wild, playful tribute,
                     Graced by the Graces, the pure,
                Holy dance of the sacred Mysteries.   335

336 Lady The Greek *korē*, a word meaning 'maiden', is frequently used to refer to Persephone, the daughter of Zeus and Demeter, who was snatched into the underworld by her uncle Hades to be his consort.

337 pork The sacrifice of a piglet formed part of the Eleusinian Mysteries and the Thesmophoria, a festival to Demeter celebrated in October (see illustration, p. 24). In one story, the swine of Eubouleus, who witnessed Persephone's abduction, were swallowed by the earth.

Exclusion (354–70)
The Mysteries were inclusive in a way not typical of Athenian society, welcoming women and men, young and old, Athenian and foreigner, but not those who had shed blood. There were levels of initiation. Aristophanes' extended joke lists others who should **stand aside**.

357 Cratinus A comic playwright who dominated the genre before Aristophanes. He seems to be representing Dionysus as patron of drama, one of whose epithets is 'devourer of bulls' (**beef-eater**), but Cratinus was also a notorious devotee of wine.

364 five per cent Thucydides in his account of 413 BC explains the financial reasons for the Athenians imposing a new tax on maritime imports and exports (7.28.4). (For **Thorycion** (363), see 383n.)

365 sponsor our enemies' ships This would not be the formal tax, the *litourgia* (see 48n), but hints that some Athenians with oligarchic leanings might be supporting Cyrus the Persian King and the Spartan fleet.

366 Hecate's handouts A reference to Cinesias (see 153n) allegedly defecating outside a building or at a cross-roads where traditional offerings of food for the poor were left at Hecate's shrines (1363n).

CHORUS OF INITIATES Lady, honoured daughter of Demeter,
How sweet the wafting savour of roasting pork.
DIONYSUS Will you keep still! There might be a bit of crackling
going.
CHORUS OF INITIATES

Come to us, lifting in your hands the burning torches,   340
Iacchus, Iacchus!
Radiant star of our nocturnal rites.
The meadow's ablaze with light.
The old men's knees are flying,   345
As they shake off the years, their sorrows
And the long passage of time
In holy tribute.
And you, blazing with brightness,   350
Lead on towards the flowery meadow-floor,
Our dancing youth, o blessed one!

Keep silence and step aside from our dances,
Any unversed in such words,
Or impure of mind,   355
Any who know not the rites of the noble Muses,
Or the steps of the dance,
Any uninitiated
In the Bacchic rites
Voiced by that beef-eater, Cratinus;
Those who delight in buffoons who quip
With a poor sense of timing;
And the man who can't resolve a hostile row,
But, ill at ease with his fellow citizen,   360
Fuels and fans their feuds,
Eyes fixed on private gain.

The magistrate who, when our city's storm-tossed,
Lines his pockets and betrays a garrison or crew;
Or, like that creep Thorycion, runs contraband from Aegina,
While creaming off the five per cent,
And traffics to Epidaurus row-lock padding, ropes and tar;   365

368 mocked The Chorus include those who can't take a joke when caricatured in the theatre but prosecute the playwright, as Cleon did to Aristophanes for his play *Babylonians* in 426 BC.

- Compare lines 357–70 with the following 'little lists':
  (1) *All people who have flabby hands and irritating laughs … all third persons who on spoiling tête-à-têtes insist … the idiot who praises, with enthusiastic tone, / All centuries but this, and every country but his own … And that singular anomaly, the lady novelist – I don't think she'd be missed* (Gilbert and Sullivan, *The Mikado*, 1885)
  (2) *All people who host chat shows and the guests what's on them too … those who have their noses pierced … men who dye their hair … traffic wardens, bankers … accountants of all kinds* (updated extracts from Eric Idle's lyrics for *The Mikado*, 1987)
- Who would be on your list?

380 the saviour The rhythm changes to something more like a march. The Initiates sing of a female **saviour**, who might be Athene, Persephone or Demeter, but it is certainly to Demeter that they pray for safety in lines 387–9.

Demeter

Demeter was goddess of grain and harvest. The *Homeric Hymn to Demeter* tells how Hades abducted her daughter Persephone as she gathered flowers. Demeter searched for her relentlessly and when she learned the truth, her grief prevented the earth from bearing fruit or grain. Eventually Zeus interceded with Hades and Persephone was allowed to return, provided she had eaten nothing. Since she had tasted a pomegranate in Hades' realm she was condemned to spend part of the year (winter) in the underworld, but brought spring and summer with her when she returned to her loving mother. The Eleusinian Mysteries may have included a re-enactment of the myth, which offers an allegory both for the seasons and for the life-cycle of grain and other plants. This story, like that of Orpheus (see **'Orpheus … Musaeus … Hesiod … Homer'**, p. 70), is appropriate to a play about descent into the underworld and the bringing back to life of a poet.

383 Thorycion The officer named and shamed at line 363 against a general backdrop of wartime corruption and profiteering.

389–91 I've lots of good jokes to tell … Worthy of your festival
Humour and playfulness abound in this Chorus. The Greek verb *paizein* – to act childishly – occurs many times. This is one of several ways in which there is overlap between the cults of Dionysus and Demeter. One feature of the procession from Athens to Eleusis was ritual insult and mockery indulged in by participants as they crossed the river Cephissus.

Or gets someone to sponsor our enemies' ships;
The poet, twirling as he sings, who adds
His own deposit to Hecate's handouts;
The politician who takes a bite out of a comic playwright's
Earnings when mocked in our traditional
Worship of Dionysus.

Yes, it's you I'm speaking to! I'll say it once and twice
And once again: stand aside from our mystic dance.   370

The rest of you, start up the singing
And our all-night revels, as befits this festival!
Now each go boldly forth
Into the flowery folds
Of meadows, stamping
And laughing, frolicking   375
And joking, after an ample feast!

Step forth, be sure to raise
Your voice in noble song
To the saviour, through whose care,   380
She says, this land of ours
Is safe for time to come,
Whatever Thorycion thinks.

Come now, and choose another song
For our fruitful queen, the goddess Demeter,
Adorning her with worshipful song   385
As the tide of your voices bursts forth!

Demeter, queen of our holy rites, stand at our side;
Keep this, your special Chorus, safe;
And safely let me play and dance
The whole day through.

I've lots of good jokes to tell
And much to say in earnest, too,
Let my mirth and jests prove   390
Worthy of your festival. Let me win
And wear your champion's crown!

Dionysus and Demeter

There is ambiguity in some of the phrases this Chorus use: **your special Chorus** (387), **your festival** (391), **your champion's crown** (392) could easily refer to the dramatic festival of Dionysus. We have already seen the partial identification of Iacchus with Dionysus (316n), himself a *friend of the Chorus*, and the potential ironic humour of the god eavesdropping on his own worshippers (315).

404 you split my sandals and tore my cloak There is a ritual element here, but the procession from Athens to Eleusis, **the distance here** (403) of 22 km, will have taken its toll on footwear and clothes.

Smut

As they near the end of their entry song the Initiates become risqué, which Dionysus clearly enjoys (415), then increasingly crude, savouring the latest scandals (416–30). Dionysus cuts short their gossip. This form of abuse, familiar in comedy at festivals of Dionysus, was a ritual part of the procession to Eleusis. At certain points the crowd would stop to chant ritual obscenities.

416 Archedemus There is a pun here on *phrastēres*, **adult teeth**, and *phrateres*, kinsmen. Being presented to one's *phratry* was a ceremony of initiation into an ancestral group; without this rite, which took place when a boy was very young at the *Apatouria*, one was an outsider. Archedemus, for all his aspirations, does not belong.

Come now! Let our songs invite here
The youthful god, your fellow companion
In the dance.

Iacchus, highly honoured one, discover
The delight of our festive song.
Come here and join us, join
The goddess. Show us
How little effort it takes
For you to cover the distance here.
Iacchus, friend of the Chorus,
Be our companion!

For you split my sandals and tore my cloak,
For a laugh, but for economy too,
And you discovered how to let us
Dance and have a bit of fun
Without us having to pay.
Iacchus, friend of the Chorus,
Be our companion!

Actually, I just took a peek at a little lass
I'd spotted – a pretty little playmate –
And, through a rip in her gown,
A little booby peeped out.
Iacchus, friend of the Chorus,
Be our companion!

DIONYSUS Somehow I've always been a fan of this sort of thing.
I'd quite like to join the Chorus – and play with her myself.
XANTHIAS Me too!

CHORUS OF INITIATES Shall we all have a laugh at Archedemus?
At seven he'd still not cut
His adult teeth.
But he cuts it with the adults now
– The crowd of stiffs above –
As leading cut-throat there.

I hear that in amongst the tombs,

395

400

405

410

415

420

422 Cleisthenes Ridiculed already for his sexual tastes (see 48, 57), his sexual desperation is suggested as the Chorus engage in a graphic flight of fancy using imagery of ritual mourning (tearing of cheeks and hair, beating of head). His friend's name is invented for obscene effect.

428 Callias Son of Hipponicus, he was an extremely wealthy Athenian whose consequent high profile in Athenian life included the office of *diadouchos* or torch-bearer in the Eleusinian procession. He appears in the works of Plato and Xenophon as someone with more money than sense and was ridiculed in Eupolis' *Flatterers*. Aristophanes has swapped two letters in the father's name to Hippocinus (it now means horse-bonker, not horse-victor).

439 Corinthian Xanthias mutters witty protests. *Coris* (bed-bug in Greek) is a frequent pun in Aristophanes. Corinth was Sparta's strongest ally in the war against Athens. The reference in Greek is more precisely to 'Zeus' son, Corinthus', who gave his name to the city, but also appears to have the proverbial meaning Pindar, *Nemean Ode* 7.105 (e.g. 'same old story', *Assembly Women* 828).

Parodying the Mysteries

It is difficult to assess the extent to which what was performed on stage resembled the Mysteries, whose initiates were sworn to secrecy. Aristophanes might have risked angering people in this *parodos* and in an earlier play, *Thesmophoriazusae* (411 BC), just as in 1791 Mozart angered those who felt their Masonic rites had been violated in his *Magic Flute*. Ten years before *Frogs* was first performed, a group of young aristocrats including Alcibiades (see *'Parodos'*, p. 24) had been charged with profaning the Mysteries, a case that had far-reaching implications for Athens (see pp. v–vii). Others implicated were Critias, Adeimantus (1514) and the orator Andocides, who defended himself against this charge more than once in his turbulent career (*On the Mysteries*). A speech attacking him (*Against Andocides*, Lysias 6) survives.

Review of *parodos* (316–459)

What have you learned about the nature of the Initiates and their rituals?
- Are they an appropriate chorus for this play?
- Consider the potential impact of pipe-music, dance and costumes on this scene.
- 'They will tell you everything you need' (161). How helpful have the Initiates been in terms of moving the plot forward? What else do they add to the play?

460 the door The Chorus have just advised Dionysus and Xanthias that they've reached Hades' front door. Aristophanes' underworld seems more like a local neighbourhood than a chthonic realm.
- Design the doorway for a stage production. Should it be impressive or ordinary?

Cleisthenes' arsehole is plucking out its hairs
And tearing its cheeks!
He was bending over and beating his head,
Crying out and screaming 425
For Bonkmeagen, whoever that is.

...And they say that Callias
– You know, Hippoknickers' son –
Went off to fight at sea, hunting pussy 430
In fitted lionskin pants.

DIONYSUS Could you possibly tell the two of us
Whereabouts Pluto lives?
We're strangers, just arrived.
CHORUS OF INITIATES No need to go further – or ask any more. 435
That's his front door you've reached, you know.
DIONYSUS Pick that up again, lad.
XANTHIAS Same old routine.
Something about this bed bugs me.
Is there a Corinthian in there?
CHORUS OF INITIATES Go now, through the goddess' holy circle, 440
Skipping through the flowery glade,
Those of you taking part in this festival,
So dear to the gods.
I will go where these girls and women 445
Pass the night in worship of the goddess,
And bear the sacred torch.
Let us go to the rose-gardens,
The meadows that blossom with flowers, 450
In our own special way,
Skipping our loveliest dance-steps,
Led on by the blessed Muses.

We alone see the sacred light and the sun, 455
We are the initiates, our ways are pious
To each and every one, strangers, guests and all.
DIONYSUS So, how should I knock on the door? 460
Come on. How do the locals knock here?

463 You're dressed like Heracles (see illustration, p. 8). In the scenes that follow, the club and lionskin provide an impenetrable disguise and ample scope for dramatic irony. Aeacus immediately believes that he is seeing the real Heracles returning to the underworld.

463 Aeacus Traditionally one of the three judges of the dead (see illustration, p. 12). In this play, he appears as an over-excitable doorman who takes disturbing pleasure in listing the punishments in store.

466 our dog Cerberus Heracles describes in the *Odyssey* how he was sent to the underworld to bring back a hound since it was thought there was no more difficult task; Hermes and Athene had escorted him (*Odyssey* 11.623–6). Homer's contemporary Hesiod names Cerberus and gives more detail; he is the second son of Echidna (**the hundred-headed viper**) and is *unspeakable, an irresistible savage with a voice of bronze, fifty-headed, shameless and powerful* (*Theogony* 310–12). In later art and literature Cerberus has two or three heads.

472 Cocytus Underworld river (see **'Homer's underworld'**, p. 10).

476 Gorgons Appearing frequently in early Greek art, to alarm the enemy or avert danger, they were three sisters with features so hideous they could turn men or monsters to stone. Medusa is the best known. **Tithrasian** is a local reference to one of the demes in Attica, while **Tartessian** (475) refers to a Greek colony in remote Spain.

486 most cowardly of gods – and men Different superlatives are used of Dionysus in Euripides' *Bacchae*, produced posthumously in 405 BC; he is *most terrible and most mild to men* (861). His presence and punishment in that play of those who fail to honour him are terrifying; he is a far cry from the sorry figure Xanthias chides and cajoles.

XANTHIAS Oh – don't waste time, just give it a go.

You're dressed like Heracles. Now act like him.

DIONYSUS Slave, slave.

AEACUS Who's this?

DIONYSUS Heracles the mighty.

AEACUS You disgusting, shameless, arrogant, brutal, totally brutal,   465
most brutallest man. You sprang on our dog Cerberus, dragged
him out and strangled him. Then you ran away, taking him with
you. Clean gone, and I was looking after him. But now you're
caught. The black-hearted rocks of Styx and the blood-stained   470
cliffs of Acheron are watching out for you; so are the dogs of
Cocytus and the hundred-headed viper who will rip your guts   475
out; the Tartessian lamprey will lock on to your ribs, and as for
your kidneys, the Tithrasian Gorgons will tear them from your
very innards, dripping blood. I'll just run off and get them.

XANTHIAS Hey, what have you done?

DIONYSUS I've made a craprifice.

XANTHIAS You ridiculous fool, get up quickly before someone sees   480
you.

DIONYSUS I can't. I feel faint. Place a sponge on my heart.

XANTHIAS Here, take it. Put it there. Where's it gone?

Golden gods! Your heart's not down there, is it?

DIONYSUS Yes: it was frightened and crept down to my bowels.   485

XANTHIAS You are the most cowardly of gods – and men.

DIONYSUS Me? I'm not a coward – I asked you for a sponge!

No other man would have done that.

XANTHIAS Oh? And what would he have done?

DIONYSUS A coward would have lain there whiffing.

But I got up, even wiped myself down.   490

XANTHIAS Oh, very brave, by Poseidon.

DIONYSUS Well I think so, by Zeus.

Weren't *you* frightened by his shouts and threats?

XANTHIAS It didn't bother me.

Dressing up

The roles of master and slave have almost been reversed already (see, e.g., 480–1). This is a pattern that becomes well established in later Greek and Roman comedy, where the clever slave often outwits his master. Xanthias steps forward with good cheer as he takes on the costume and spirit of the great hero.

- Do you think an Athenian audience would have been glad to see the 'under-dog' enjoying his day, alarmed at the thought of a slave bettering his master, or simply amused by the scenario?

501 whipping boy from Melite Dionysus deflates Xanthias using a put-down that may suggest that in the lionskin he looks less like Heracles and more like Callias (428), thought to live in **Melite**.

Heracles and the maid

Heracles was celebrated for his great appetites when it came to food, drink and other sensual pleasures. In vase paintings epic feasts are illustrated alongside his epic feats. When Heracles joins the celebrations at the end of Aristophanes' *Birds*, he volunteers to help with the cooking. *Tasting, more likely*, says the new ruler of Cloudcuckooland as he refuses the offer. Heracles' womanising leads directly to his death in Sophocles' *Trachiniae*, where his wife Deaneira tries to turn his eyes from the new, younger woman Iole by using a love-potion that turns out to be a deadly poison. The maid and Persephone (the **goddess**, 504) clearly have warmer memories of Heracles' last visit than the enraged Aeacus has. After initial reluctance, 'Xanthacles' succumbs to the maid's offers and Dionysus regrets the change of role.

529 I need a witness! Xanthias' cry, a reminder of the litigious nature of the Athenians and their obsession with law-courts (see *Wasps* and *Clouds* 207–8), suggests that Dionysus becomes physical in his attempts to get the costume back.

DIONYSUS Well, then, since you are so courageous and full of
    spirit, swap places with me. Take this club and lionskin, if you   495
    really aren't a scaredy-guts. In return, I'll be your porter.

XANTHIAS Come on, then, quickly. I don't need persuading.
    Just look – not Heracles, but Xanthacles!
    Now see if I am as cowardly and lacking in spirit as you.   500

DIONYSUS Well, by Zeus, aren't you the whipping boy from Melite?
    Come on, then, let me pick up this kit here.

MAID O Heracles, darling, you have arrived. Come on in.
    The goddess heard you were coming and had some fresh bread
    baked straightaway; two or three pots of lentil soup are bubbling   505
    away and she's barbecued a whole ox and toasted some
    honey-cakes. Come on in.

XANTHIAS Lovely, but you're too kind.

MAID By Apollo, I won't let you go. She is also simmering some
    chicken breasts, preparing desserts and mixing some   510
    wonderfully sweet wine. Come on in and join me.

XANTHIAS Very nice, but…

MAID Don't be silly. I'm not letting you go now. Plus there's this girl
    inside for you who plays the pipes – very juicy – and several
    dancing girls as well.   515

XANTHIAS Did you say dancing girls?

MAID They're nice and young and freshly plucked.
    Just go on in. The cook is just about to slice the fish and your
    table is ready.

XANTHIAS Off you go, then. Quick as you can, tell those dancing
    girls inside that the boss is coming.   520
    This slave will accompany me and bring my things.

DIONYSUS Hey, hold on. You weren't taking me seriously when I
    disguised you as Heracles, for a laugh?
    Stop talking nonsense, Xanthias.
    Just pick up the bags and bring them.   525

XANTHIAS What? You only just gave me these. And now you are
    intending to take them back?

DIONYSUS Not intending. I'm doing it. Give me the lionskin.

XANTHIAS I need a witness! I appeal to the gods!

531 Alcmene Zeus slept with Alcmene disguised as her husband, Amphitryon and fathered Heracles. Zeus' wife Hera prevented him from becoming the great king that had been predicted by speeding up the birth of another child, Eurystheus. Heracles had to perform his 12 labours for this master. Hera ruthlessly afflicted Heracles with a madness that made him kill his first wife Megaera and their children. This is the subject of Euripides' play *Heracles*.

Interlude

The Chorus reflect on Dionysus' change of plan while making a political point. Politicians always struggle to present U-turns convincingly and risk being mocked for them. Dionysus has decided to reverse his previous decision to let Xanthias play Heracles. In the first lyric stanza the Chorus appear to praise him for this until the sting comes at the end of their verse. Dionysus' fantasy suggests other reasons for his change of heart.

541 Theramenes A powerful politician at this time (see also 967–8), Theramenes was involved in many of the important events of the years leading to his death in 404/403 BC. He helped to establish and then overthrow the Four Hundred, the oligarchic government imposed on Athens in 411 BC (Aristotle, *Athenian Constitution* 29–33); he commanded a ship at the Battle of Arginusae in 406 BC and was instrumental in bringing the generals to trial for failing to collect their dead (see **'Arginusae, 406 BC'**, p. 50). He negotiated terms of final peace with the Spartan commander Lysander and was one of the Thirty Tyrants in the post-war regime of 404 BC. His views were more moderate than, e.g., those of Critias (another of the Thirty, a friend of Alcibiades and admirer of Sparta) and this led to his execution. (See *Time line*, pp. 112–113, and *Background to the story*, pp. v–vii).

545 chick-pea A bizarre euphemism. Masturbation is commonly referred to in Greek comedy (e.g. *Knights* 21–9, *Clouds* 734).

548 chorus / Of teeth This metaphor suggesting that a row of teeth are like a ring of dancers has particular force as Dionysus is in feisty dialogue with his own chorus here.

Blasphemy?

- Do you find the comic representation of Dionysus in this play surprising or disturbing? Is it blasphemous?
- How does it compare with Euripides' treatment of Dionysus in his *Bacchae* (see 486n) and the image on p. 40?
- What does it tell you about the nature of Dionysus' cult and the Athenian theatre?
- Can you think of a parallel for this disrespectful representation of a god in any contemporary religion?

DIONYSUS What gods? How stupid and senseless – the idea that
    you, a slave and a mere mortal, could be the son of Alcmene!   530

XANTHIAS I don't care. Here, take them. You'll probably want them
    back sometime, and what the god wants …

CHORUS OF INITIATES You can tell a man
                    Of sound heart and mind   535
                    Who's well travelled.
                    He always rolls to the
                    Safe side of the ship
                    Rather than standing
                    Like a formal portrait,
                    Holding his pose.
                    Taking a U-turn
                    Towards an easier position
                    Is the mark of a sharp cookie,   540
                    A true Theramenes.

DIONYSUS   Would it be all that amusing
                    If Xanthias – a slave –
                    All tangled up
                    In luxury blankets and
                    Snogging a dancing girl,
                    Asks for a potty
                    And looking at him there,
                    I start buffing my chick-pea;   545
                    So he, being a bit of a lad,
                    Sees me, clenches his fist,
                    Smacks me on the jaw
                    And wipes the smile
                    Off my chorus
                    Of teeth?

Cleophrades Painter, Dionysus, c. 650 BC.

Heracles and the innkeepers

Some jokes work well because the audience can guess what's coming. Dionysus plays 'Heracles' for the third encounter, this time with two angry female innkeepers. One is called **Plathane** (550), a common name in Athens. The impression of a suburban underworld with houses and places to stay (see 112–15, 460n) is sustained.

558 high-heeled boots (*kothornoi*) Actors wore these to make them more visible. Masks were originally worn for the same reason. Dionysus is wearing them, like his yellow gown, as god of drama. A lot of self-reflective comedy is generated by dressing up in this play.

569–70 Cleon...Hyperbolus The women call to their defence two nasty, dead politicians to attack the villain. Aristophanes has a vicious go at both popular leaders (demagogues) in *Knights*, 424 BC. **Cleon**, presented as a loud and aggressive politician, attempted to prosecute Aristophanes (see 368n, 577). He was killed in action in 422 BC, but Aristophanes continued to resurrect old jokes long after his death. **Hyperbolus**, whom the comic poet Eupolis attacked in his *Maricas*, 421 BC, was ostracised in about 416 BC and killed in 411 BC.

574 that pit The word is *barathron*, an incongruous reference to a pit behind the Acropolis in Athens where criminals (and Persian ambassadors, see Herodotus 7.133) were thrown.

PANDOCEUTRIA Plathane, Plathane, come here. This is the bastard
who came into our inn one day and ate sixteen of our loaves. 550

PLATHANE By god, that's the very man!

XANTHIAS Someone's heading for trouble.

PANDOCEUTRIA And not only that – twenty braised steaks worth
half an obol each.

XANTHIAS He'll pay for it now.

PANDOCEUTRIA And an awful lot of garlic. 555

DIONYSUS Complete nonsense, madam. You don't know what
you're talking about.

PANDOCEUTRIA So you weren't expecting me to recognise you
again in those high-heeled boots? Well? And I haven't even
mentioned all that pickled fish – yet.

PLATHANE Nor all that fresh cheese he ate up, you poor thing 560
– baskets and all.

PANDOCEUTRIA And then when I was working out the cost, he
shot me a nasty look and started bellowing.

XANTHIAS That's him. That's how he behaves all the time.

PANDOCEUTRIA Then he drew his sword as if he'd gone crazy.

PLATHANE O heavens, dear me! 565

PANDOCEUTRIA We were both terrified. We jumped up and ran
straight upstairs. But he was off. He charged out, bedding and all.

XANTHIAS Oh, that's just like him.

PANDOCEUTRIA Well, what could we do? Go and call that man
Cleon. He'll protect us.

PLATHANE And you, if you see Hyperbolus, get him for me, 570
then we can batter him!

PANDOCEUTRIA O monstrous gullet, I'd like to get a rock and
smash in those teeth of yours that tucked into my wares.

PLATHANE And I'd like to hurl you down that pit.

PANDOCEUTRIA I'd like to get a big, curved knife and cut that 575
throat of his out for gulping down all those sausages.
Right. I'm going to get Cleon. He'll have you in court today and
will wring every last drop out of you.

583 a slave and a mere mortal Xanthias throws Dionysus' words at 531 back at him.

586–7 my wife, and my children Dionysus is reduced to pleading with his slave by swearing an oath. Gods usually swear by the river Styx, but Dionysus chooses a domestic oath that feels suspicious, given the lack of evidence of a wife or children in the play. In traditional myth, Dionysus takes as his consort King Minos' daughter Ariadne and has children by her.

588 Archedemus This reference undercuts the seriousness of Dionysus' oath. Archedemus was ridiculed as the ambitious outsider (417). He brought charges of embezzlement against Erasinides, one of the generals at Arginusae (see 1196 and **'Arginusae, 406 BC'**, p. 50).

Equal encouragement?
The Chorus' song and Xanthias' response mirror the form of the exchange at 533–49. In both the Chorus try to put heart into the hero, who is now the slave, not the god.
- Do you detect any favouritism in the Chorus' words of encouragement?
- Who do you think is more successful at playing Heracles, Dionysus or Xanthias?

605 this dog-napper Aeacus has returned with reinforcements to make Heracles pay for his former crime. This time Xanthias is not so lucky to be dressed as Heracles.

606 Someone's in trouble Dionysus echoes Xanthias' words at 552.

DIONYSUS May I die most horribly, if I don't love you, Xanthias.

XANTHIAS I know what you're thinking and you can stop it now.   580
Stop it. Don't say anything. I don't want to be Heracles.

DIONYSUS No, of course not, Xanthy Wanthy.

XANTHIAS And how *could* I be the son of Alcmene? 'I, a slave and
a mere mortal!'

DIONYSUS I know, I know you're angry, and you're right to be. And
if you hit me, I wouldn't blame you. But if I take the disguise   585
from you ever, ever again, may I, my wife, and my children – and
poor, gummy-eyed Archedemus – be utterly destroyed.

XANTHIAS OK. I accept your oath and the costume on these terms.

CHORUS OF INITIATES   Your task
Now you've got back   590
The costume you had before
Is to find that old spirit again,
And once more look fierce.
Remember the god
You've made yourself look like.
If you are caught
Sounding silly or soft   595
You won't have a chance,
You'll be stuck with the baggage again.

XANTHIAS   Gents, your advice is not bad,
In fact I'd just had the same thought.
If anything good comes of this
He'll try to take it all back   600
– I know that well.
Even so, I will show myself
Brave of spirit and sour of look.
And I think I might need to,
Because I can hear
A racket at the door.

AEACUS Tie this dog-napper up quickly so we can punish him.   605
Do it!

DIONYSUS Someone's in trouble.

XANTHIAS Don't you come near me, you bastard.

608–9 Ditylus, Sceblyas, Phartphace Aeacus calls in his heavies. Their names sound foreign and they may have been represented as Scythian archers, the only form of official law enforcement in Athens. The name of the third thug is really Pardocas, perhaps suggesting the Greek verb *perdomai* (fart).

610 Dreadful! Dionysus shows himself a true coward here as he sides with the stronger force against his own slave and comrade.

Torture

A casual reference in *Clouds* 620 suggests torture was routine, although records of trials suggest it was restricted to slaves or foreigners and was not especially frequent in Athens (see also 624n).

621 leeks This joke is a good example of bathos and works well because it's absurd; hitting a man with a leek is demeaning and silly, rather than painful.

624 compensation Aeacus is observing the Athenian legal niceties of torturing a slave. A prosecutor or defendant was expected to have the permission of the owner, who might attend the process (see 626), and to recompense him for damage to his property. Xanthias returns his master's disloyalty (see 610) with interest, relishing the reversal of the status quo and co-operating fully with the torture of his slave.

A second *agōn*

Dionysus was last in direct competition with the Chorus of Frogs (209–69), where he successfully rowed across the lake and claimed to have silenced them. In this contest he should have a clear advantage over Xanthias because he, unlike his slave, actually is a god.

AEACUS You going to fight me, then? Ditylus, Sceblyas, Phartphace, come here and rough him up.

DIONYSUS Dreadful! This man steals someone else's things and 610 then starts brawling?

AEACUS Monstrous.

DIONYSUS Yes. Wicked, terrible!

XANTHIAS By Zeus, if I ever came here or stole anything of yours, I'm ready to die for it. Tell you what: I'll make you a fair offer. 615 Take this slave of mine and torture him. And if you find me in the wrong, take me and kill me.

AEACUS How shall I torture him?

XANTHIAS Any way you like. Tie him to a ladder, hang him up, lash him with whips, flay him, stretch him, pour vinegar up his 620 nostrils, pile hot bricks on him, whatever you want. Except leeks. Don't hit him with a leek – not even a little one.

AEACUS Sounds reasonable. And if I damage your slave when I beat him, I can offer you something as compensation.

XANTHIAS Oh, I don't need that. Take him away and torture him. 625

AEACUS Over there, then, so he can look you in the eye when he speaks. And you, put that baggage down quickly and let's have 630 no more of your lies.

DIONYSUS I appeal! Don't torture me. I'm a god. If you don't listen, you'll have only yourself to blame.

AEACUS What are you saying?

DIONYSUS Immortal. That's what I am. Dionysus, son of Zeus. This man is a slave.

AEACUS Do you hear that?

XANTHIAS I certainly did and he should be beaten all the more. If he *is* a god, he won't feel it.

DIONYSUS What about this? Since you claim to be a god yourself, 635 why don't you get the same beating as me?

XANTHIAS A fair argument. Whichever of us you see crying or pleading first, he's the one you should reckon isn't a god.

AEACUS What a decent chap you are. A very fair solution. 640 Strip off, then.

XANTHIAS How will you make our torture fair?

AEACUS Easy. A blow for you, a blow for him.

The beating

The Greek text rarely includes stage directions (see **'Stage direction'**, p. 24). In performance a director needs to work out when the blows fall. Aeacus starts with Xanthias and beats him three times (645–6, 649, 657). Dramatic irony is at work here; the audience keep expecting Aeacus to work out what's going on, but he is no sleuth, it seems.

649 *Attatai!!!!!* The Greek *attatai* is a common exclamation of pain or distress. The festival of Heracles took place in Diomea, a *deme* south of the Acropolis. Perhaps 'Xanthacles' is feigning anxiety about missing his festival.

653 men on horseback Dionysus tries to pass his exclamation off as if it were one of excitement, perhaps at seeing a procession or military force setting out. Aeacus isn't quite convinced, so Dionysus invents the **onions** (654), presumably because the pain has brought tears to his eyes. This could be consistent with his first story since onions were a staple part of army rations.

Frogs *(adapted by Stephen Sondheim and Burt Shelove), Point Park Conservatory Theater, Pittsburgh, 2007; directed by Scott Wise. Thomas Sullivan as Heracles and Dale Spollett as Dionysus.*

XANTHIAS Excellent. Watch closely now; see if I move at all.
Have you hit me yet?

AEACUS No, by Zeus. 645

XANTHIAS I didn't think so.

AEACUS Now I'll go up to this chap and hit him.

DIONYSUS When exactly?

AEACUS I've already hit you.

DIONYSUS How come I didn't even sneeze?

AEACUS I don't know. I'll try again on him.

XANTHIAS Please get on with it.
Attatai!!!!!

AEACUS What do you mean – *attatai*? Surely you're not in pain? 650

XANTHIAS No, by Zeus. I had a thought. *Atta-at*…At what time
will the festival of Heracles in Diomea take place?

AEACUS A pious man. You must come again. Back to this chap.

DIONYSUS Oooh, oooh!

AEACUS What is it?

DIONYSUS I see men on horseback.

AEACUS Then why are you crying?

DIONYSUS It's the smell of onions.

AEACUS Nothing else? 655

DIONYSUS No, nothing. Nothing's bothering me.

AEACUS Then it's back over to this one.

XANTHIAS Oh, oh!

AEACUS What is it?

XANTHIAS Could you pull this splinter out for me?

AEACUS What *is* all this? Back to him again.

659 Delos and Delphi The island of Delos was the birthplace of Apollo and Artemis. Delphi was the site of Apollo's famous oracle.

661 Hipponax Dionysus quotes the 6th-century poet at 659 and a line from Sophocles' *Laocoon* at 665–6.

665 *headland of Aegeus* Returning from a dangerous mission to kill the Minotaur in Crete, Theseus failed to signal his triumph to his father Aegeus, king of Athens, by changing the sails from black to white. Believing his son dead, Aegeus threw himself into the sea.

And the winner is…

There is no final result, because Aeacus confesses himself baffled and thinks up an easier way of getting to the truth (670–2). However, Xanthias has shown superior cunning and, arguably, courage. He gleefully diverts what should have been his fourth blow into an extra painful **thwack** for his master (662).

PARABASIS (674–737)

The *parabasis* occurs at the midpoint of the play, providing a change of tone and atmosphere. The Chorus often step out of character and the Chorus leader (*coryphaeus*) addresses the audience directly, airing views on anything from what the audience think of the show so far and why this play deserves to win, to completely unrelated news and scandals of the day. The task they take on, to **instruct the city** (686–7), becomes an important theme as the role and importance of the poet is discussed and analysed (see 1010, 1055, 1420–1).

675 Come, Muse The lyric ode that opens the *parabasis* is balanced in a lighter vein by 706–17. After seeking inspiration from the Muse, the Chorus flatter the **clever** audience as a way of unifying 'The people vs Cleophon'.

678 Cleophon (see *Background to the story*, pp. v–vii) He was an opponent of peace with Sparta and the most prominent demagogue of his day once democracy was restored after the brief rule of the Four Hundred in 411 BC (see also 140n, 1504n). The Chorus hint at Cleophon's Thracian mother, his ambition (**keener to win**, 678), the style of his rhetoric and his duplicity. A **tie** (685) would usually mean acquittal. Cleophon was tried for treason in 405 BC. His condemnation and execution paved the way for Theramenes (541n) to negotiate peace in 404 BC.

689 Phrynichus Son of Stratonides and one of the Four Hundred. A decree was passed after his fall in 410 BC labelling all officials of the fallen regime 'enemies of Athens'. Using a wrestling metaphor, the Chorus advocate clemency for those who were tricked or bullied into following his lead.

DIONYSUS *Aaah-pollo! – Lord of Delos and Delphi!*

XANTHIAS He felt pain! Didn't you hear? 660

DIONYSUS No, I didn't. I was just remembering a verse of
Hipponax.

XANTHIAS You are getting nowhere. Just thwack him under the
ribs!

AEACUS Right, by Zeus. Stick your stomach out, now.

DIONYSUS Po ... ... sei ... ... don!

XANTHIAS Someone's hurting!

DIONYSUS *... lord of the headland of Aegeus, and the depths of the* 665
silvery sea.

AEACUS By Demeter, I can't find out yet which of you is the god.
Just go inside. The master himself will identify you – and 670
Persephone, since they are both gods themselves.

DIONYSUS Well said. I just wish you'd thought of that before you
started hitting me.

CHORUS OF INITIATES Come, Muse, attend our sacred dancing, 675
Come, take pleasure in our song.
You'll see here a mass of people,
A clever audience, thousands strong,
And keener to win than Cleophon.
In his babbling, two-tongued mouth
Perched upon a foreign leaf
There sits a Thracian swallow;
Twittering like thunder, 680
Warbling its mournful song,
The nightingale's lament:
'I'll die, if it's a tie.' 685

CHORUS LEADER It is right for a holy chorus to encourage and
instruct the city in what's good for it. So our first policy is that all
citizens should be treated as equals, free from fear. And if
anyone has been tripped or thrown by one of Phrynichus' moves
and made a mistake, I say their slip should be overlooked and,
once they've explained themselves, the slate wiped clean. 690

694 Plataean citizenship The Spartans destroyed Athens' ally Plataea in 427 BC. Like slaves who fought at Arginusae, refugees who fled to Athens were given citizenship with some restrictions (e.g. they could vote and own slaves, but couldn't be archons or priests).

Arginusae, 406 BC

This Athenian naval victory was still the 'headline story' in Athens at the time of *Frogs* because of the controversy over the generals' conduct and their trial in late October / early November 406 BC (see *Background to the story*, pp. v–vii, and 1197n). The Chorus draw a rhetorical contrast between the new security of former slaves and the insecurity of experienced naval officers, like those who fought in the sea-battle. They appeal to the common sense and humanity of the audience in emotive language, both in the context of **that one disaster** (699–700) and in the more general context of any naval allies.

710 Cleigenes Little is known of this minor political figure, who is made to sound a nasty piece of work.

Coins (718–34) (see illustration, below)

The Chorus introduce an analogy between the quality of political leaders and of coinage. The Athenians were famed for their pure silver 'Owls' after the discovery of silver mines in Laurium before the Persian Wars, but the Spartan occupation of Decelea had stopped the mining of an already diminished seam. Financial pressures of the long war with Sparta forced the Athenians in 407/406 BC to use gold from their temples. The silver and gold coins are of true quality, like the **finest men**. War also led to a downgrading of currency: base metals (copper/ bronze) plated with silver came into circulation. They look promising, but should not be trusted. Base types would presumably include the likes of Cleophon (678n); it is harder to identify the **finest men**. Those **raised to wrestle and dance and sing** (727–8) suggests aristocrats of elite birth and education. The foremost was Alcibiades, who came with his own problems (see **'Parodying the Mysteries'**, p. 32). The phrase **go for gold** (734) more literally means 'use the best'.

Emergency stater of Athens, 406 BC.

Next, I say that no man in our city should be without rights. It's a
disgrace that, on the one hand, men who fought in a single
sea-battle received Plataean citizenship, stopped being slaves and
became masters – not that I personally have any objection to   695
that; in fact, I'm all for it; it's about the only sensible thing you've
done! It's just that you should do more: men who've fought at sea
with you many times, as did their fathers, men close in kin to
you, should be forgiven that one disaster, should they ask. Let
your anger go, show your natural wisdom. Let us gladly claim as   700
brothers and honoured citizens all who fight with us at sea.
If on this matter we stand aloof and proud, especially when our
city's fate depends on the sea, at a later date we'll not seem quite
so smart.   705

      If my view's right, one man's habit
    Of a lifetime points to trouble ahead for him.
  It won't be long. The monkey's under suspicion,
  Little Primate Cleigenes, the nastiest bath-man   710
On the block of master-mixers who cut their soda
    And white-clay with ash and dust. He's
      Running out of time, and seeing this,
        He can't rest easy, in case   715
          When out for a walk
          Without his stick
           – and drunk –
           He's stripped.

I've often thought our city treats her finest citizens like her
vintage coins and the new gold. These coins are first class,
nothing fake, the only ones true-minted, guaranteed by their   720
pure ring, accepted everywhere by Greek and foreigner alike.
But rather than them, we use these base bronze things, struck
yesterday or the day before with a feeble stamp. It's the same with 725
politicians. The ones we know to be noble, wise and just, the
finest men, raised to wrestle and dance and sing, these men we
chuck aside. Instead, it's the base-metalled, copper-topped   730
foreigners and criminals we rely on for everything, the scum of

733 scapegoats The Greek *pharmakos* means 'remedy'. Two scapegoats were ritually beaten and driven out of the city, presumably to their deaths, as a purification rite at the Thargelia each May.

Review of the *parabasis*

- A decree was passed formally commending this *parabasis* in autumn 405 BC. What do you find admirable in it?
- How coherent are the views expressed?
- Can you draw any conclusions about the politics of Aristophanes and/or the Athenian audience from this *parabasis*?

Slave talk

Xanthias and another *oiketēs* (household slave) serving in the house of Hades (also known as **Pluto**, 765) open the second half of the play with another generic scene familiar to a modern audience (see p. 2): two workers grumble about their treatment and find satisfaction in getting back at 'management' in petty ways. They speak irreverently of their masters and of other gods (740, 750, 756). At least one contemporary writer remarks on the liberal conduct and treatment of some slaves: *Slaves in Athens lead a most undisciplined life; one may not strike them, nor will a slave step aside for you ... in the matter of free speech we have put slaves and free men on equal terms* ('Old Oligarch' 1.10). Most members of the audience would be familiar with the challenges and anxieties of living alongside slaves – some of them aired in this comic scene where, as a plausible plot device to explain the **racket inside** (758), an indiscreet slave shares the gossip with **outsiders** (753).

Aeschylus

There were strong grounds for acclaiming Aeschylus (*c*. 525–456 BC) **supreme in his craft** (770) (but see **'Sophocles'**, p. 54). After his first dramatic victory in 484 BC (in his early 40s) he went on to win a further 12 times in Athens in the 26 years to 458 BC, when his extant trilogy the *Oresteia* was first performed. Aeschylus' life spanned a period of dramatic political change: the end of rule by the 'tyrants' Peisistratus and his sons, the reforms of Cleisthenes and establishment in Athens of radical democracy, the Persian Wars in which Aeschylus himself fought, and the subsequent growth of Athenian power. Lines 807–9 suggest an hauteur that contrasts with Euripides' more democratic views (see 952ff). Aeschylus died at Gela in Sicily, killed – according to one popular story – by an eagle dropping a tortoise on the poet's bald head, mistaking it for a stone. What is believed to be his epitaph boasts not of his poetic triumphs but of the part he played in the Battle of Marathon in 490 BC (see 1298n).

the earth, the latest arrivals that the city would never have used 730
before – not even as scapegoats. Now's the time, you silly fools,
to change your ways and go for gold again. If all works well, it'll
make good sense – but even if you slip, whatever happens, 735
anyone of sense will see, it's a fine bit of timber from which
you're hanging!

SLAVE By Zeus the saviour, that master of yours is a decent fellow!

XANTHIAS Why wouldn't he be? All he cares about is boozing and
bonking. 740

SLAVE To think, he didn't beat you when you answered back, saying
you were the master when you're just a slave!

XANTHIAS He'd have been sorry if he had!

SLAVE The sign of a true slave. You've just done what I love doing.

XANTHIAS And what's that? Go on, tell me. 745

SLAVE Every time I curse my master behind his back, I feel like I'm
in heaven.

XANTHIAS And what about having a grumble when you get
outside after a sound beating?

SLAVE Oh, yes, I like that too!

XANTHIAS And a bit of snooping?

SLAVE God, there's nothing better!

XANTHIAS And, Zeus protect us, listening in to everything your 750
masters say?

SLAVE It drives me crazy!

XANTHIAS Then passing on the gossip to outsiders?

SLAVE Who, me? Orgasmic, by Zeus, every time!

XANTHIAS Give me your hand, by Phoebus Apollo. Here's a kiss for 755
you, and one for me. And now, by Zeus the old rogue, tell me
what is all this racket inside? This shouting and abuse?

SLAVE It's Aeschylus and Euripides.

XANTHIAS Wow.

SLAVE There is excitement, great excitement among the corpses –
and great unrest. 760

XANTHIAS Why is that?

SLAVE There's a law down here. For all the most important crafts
involving skill, the supreme artist receives free meals in the civic
hall and a seat next to Pluto himself... 765

762–3 the most important crafts A craft or *technē* was one of a wide range of skills, from shepherding to sculpting. The poetic/theatrical craft enjoyed higher status in 5th-century Athens than in most societies today and was widely accessible for citizens to appreciate through civic festivals.

764 free meals In Plato's *Apology* Socrates alienates the jury who have condemned him to death. Those convicted were allowed to propose an alternative penalty, and he suggests meals at public expense in the *prytaneion* (36d7), the **civic hall** (764) central to the activities of the *boulē* (council). Free meals were the way Athenians could demonstrate their collective gratitude to benefactors such as victorious generals and Olympic champions.

Euripides
A number of characteristics begin to emerge in this caricature of Euripides: his arguments are slippery and have easy appeal with the masses. This picture is consistent with the one painted in *Clouds*, where Euripides, born about forty years after Aeschylus, appeals as a poet to Pheidippides and the younger generation, but not to his father Strepsiades and his friends (1366–72). Many of the polarities in that play between modern and old-fashioned, liberal and conservative, impious and pious, are explored in the second half of *Frogs*. Here Euripides appeals to the lowest common denominator, rather like the demagogic Paphlagonian and Sausage-seller in Aristophanes' *Knights*.

Sophocles
The dignified picture presented in lines 788–94 contrasts with that of Euripides. Sophocles is shown to be a modest and moderating force. Sophocles (*c*. 496–406 BC) enjoyed a long and highly successful civic and poetic career. He won over twenty dramatic victories, including 18 at the City Dionysia, and was never voted third. Some time after his death he was honoured with a hero-cult, like that prophesied for Oedipus at Colonus in his posthumous play of 401 BC. See also Index.

791 Cleidemides Nothing else is known of the context in which Cleidemides chose to **sit in reserve**.

797 their poetry will be placed in the balance The use of scales as a means of determining truth is an ancient idea found in the Egyptian *Book of the Dead* and Mycenaean art. In the *Iliad*, Zeus holds out scales with the lives of two warriors balanced to see whose destiny will fall. Scales were also commonly used for commerce (799). They are eventually brought out in this poetic contest at line 1365. Other mathematical instruments mentioned (800–2), such as those admired in *Clouds* (200ff), are not actually used.

XANTHIAS I see.

SLAVE …until someone else even cleverer at his art arrives. At that point he must give way.

XANTHIAS So what is it that's disturbed Aeschylus?

SLAVE He's held the throne of tragedy, since he's supreme in his craft.

770

XANTHIAS And who has it now?

SLAVE When Euripides came down, he began to show off to the villains and muggers, the father-murderers and thieves – there are an awful lot of them in Hades. They listened to his arguments, his twists and turns and dodges and went completely mad, thinking that he was so clever. Then he got all excited, and claimed the throne where Aeschylus was sitting.

775

XANTHIAS Wasn't he booted off?

SLAVE God, no. The crowd kept yelling for a trial to see who was the more skilful artist.

780

XANTHIAS That bunch of villains?

SLAVE God, yes – their cries reached heaven!

XANTHIAS Did Aeschylus have no other supporters?

SLAVE There's not much good down here – or out there either.

XANTHIAS So what's Pluto planning to do?

SLAVE Arrange a contest straight away, a trial, and cross-examine them on their skill.

785

XANTHIAS Why hasn't Sophocles claimed the throne as well?

SLAVE That's just him, by Zeus. When he came down, he kissed Aeschylus and shook his hand. Aeschylus offered him the throne, but he's intending to do a Cleidemides and sit in reserve. If Aeschylus wins, he'll stay put; if not, he's said he'll match his skill against Euripides in a contest.

790

XANTHIAS Then it's really going to happen?

795

SLAVE Yes – in just a little while. And awesome events will take their course: their poetry will be placed in the balance.

XANTHIAS What? They're going to weigh up tragedy like a lump of meat?

SLAVE Yes, and get out their rulers and word-measures, their set-squares…

800

XANTHIAS For making bricks?

810 your master, for his experience As god of theatre, Dionysus is the obvious candidate for the role of judge in the imminent contest.

- How do the slaves show their support for Aeschylus in lines 737–812? Why do you think they side with him?

The Chorus of Initiates act like compères, introducing and rallying the contestants. They use powerful battle imagery, as if this were a Homeric duel, including the frequent Homeric compound *koruthaiolos* to evoke the **flash** of **helmets** (818). Similes likening the fighting strength and spirit of men to that of bulls (804), lions or boars, common in the *Iliad* (e.g. 4.253, 5.136), are suggested in the imagery here as Euripides sharpens his **tusk** (815) or Aeschylus' **mane** (821) bristles. There are also echoes of chariot, naval and equestrian warfare – e.g. **Linch-pins** (819), **planks** (825), **galloping** (820), **bit** (827). The two contestants are not named, but are clearly differentiated. Aeschylus, introduced with Zeus' epithet the **Thunderer**, appears in lines 814–17 and 822–5 and Euripides in lines 819–20 and 826–9.

- Is there any suggestion in this passage of which side, if any, the Chorus support?

First appearances
Expectations of how these two characters will look and behave have been raised by the words of the slaves and the Chorus, but their actual appearance is a dramatic opportunity.

- How might these characters look and sound in a modern production? Consider costume, hair, make-up, voice, physical build, mannerisms. Which modern actor would suit each part?
- How might the transition from outside the house of Hades to the argument happening inside be managed? Consider music, lighting, scenery, special effects.

SLAVE ...their compasses and wedges. Euripides says that he will
    test out the tragedies word by word.

XANTHIAS I guess Aeschylus is taking this badly?

SLAVE Yes, he lowered his head and gave a look like a bull.

XANTHIAS So who'll be judging this? 805

SLAVE Ah – that was tricky. They found there was a shortage of
    intelligent people. Aeschylus never got on with the Athenians.

XANTHIAS Probably thought most of them were crooks.

SLAVE And he regarded the rest as hopeless judges of poetic talent.
    Then they turned to your master, for his experience in the art. 810
    Anyway, let's go in. When our masters come under pressure, we
    take the rap.

CHORUS OF INITIATES Deadly the rage the Thunderer will feel
      When he sees his rival whetting his razor-sharp tusk. 815
          That's when he'll roll his eyes in a fit
             Of terrible madness.
     There will be strife, as helmets with soaring crests flash.
      Linch-pins and neatly carved concepts will shatter
     As the consummate craftsman deflects from himself
           The galloping words of attack. 820
      With the spiky crest of his shaggy mane bristling,
He'll give a terrible scowl and, bellowing loudly, hurl forth riveted
        Phrases, wrenching them off like planks
            In a Titanic blast. 825
   And then *his* smooth tongue unfurls, forming phrases
  And testing out meaning, champing at the indignant bit,
      Picking away at the words he's split 'til it's all
           Puff and nonsense.

EURIPIDES I won't give up the throne. Don't tell me what to do. 830
    I claim to be a greater artist than him.

DIONYSUS Aeschylus, why are you silent? You hear what he's
    saying.

EURIPIDES He'll make a grand opening, gesticulating portentously,
    just as he does in each of his tragedies.

DIONYSUS My dear chap, don't be too cocky. 835

840 grocer's sprout Jibes at Euripides' background are frequent in Aristophanes (see 941), in particular the slur that his mother Cleito once sold vegetables (e.g. *Thesmophoriazusae* 387).

846 a black ram Dionysus predicts a violent storm, developing the metaphor of Aeschylus as **Thunderer** (814) with images of **tornado** (848), **hailstorm** (852) and the **oak on fire** (859). The sacrifice of a black sheep was traditionally offered to appease storm gods.

849–50 cribber … unholy marriages Aeschylus loftily accuses his rival of using others' work (see 944) and of introducing scandalous material, such as Phaedra's passion for her husband's son (see 1046–53).

855 *Telephus* Euripides' production of 438 BC is parodied extensively by Aristophanes in *Acharnians* and *Thesmophoriazusae* (see also *Frogs* 864). In the complex plot Telephus learns that only the spear that wounded him can cure him; he petitions his enemy Achilles in disguise as a crippled beggar wearing rags (see 841–2, 846).

856 Let's have a civilised debate Dionysus sounds like a modern politician or someone hosting a contemporary discussion panel. Euripides' response, **bite or be bitten** (860), suggests a dog fight.

Euripides' works
Of Euripides' plays 19 survive complete (see *Time line*, pp. 112–13), not including the four mentioned here. Fragments survive of other plays, including *Telephus* (see 855n), *Meleager* and *Cretans* (see 849, 1356n).

860 lyrics Lyric passages refer to passages sung with musical accompaniment, not the words of a song. These include choral odes, sung dialogue (e.g. 971–1003) and solo performance, like the **monodies** mentioned in 849 and dealt with in Round 3 of the contest (1331–63).

A joke
Aeschylus delivers a rather good punch-line in 868. Homer's epic works are archetypal examples of immortal poetry, but drama was more ephemeral, originally written for a single performance and most of it now lost. A decree in Athens permitted revivals of Aeschylus' works and contributed to the eventual establishment of a canon of works preserved for posterity (see **'Euripides'**, p. 6).

EURIPIDES I know him and saw through him long ago – a crude craftsman, a stubborn brute – uncontrolled, unbridled, incontinent. A ponderous, bragging bundle of boasts.

AESCHYLUS Indeed, you grocer's sprout? So that's what you think   840
of me, you gossip-gathering, beggar-begetting, ripped-rag-monger? You won't repeat this with impunity.

DIONYSUS Steady, Aeschylus. Watch you don't boil your bollocks in your fury.

AESCHYLUS I'll not stop until I've utterly exposed this man   845
for the cocky cripple-monger he really is.

DIONYSUS A ram, slaves, get me a black ram. A tornado is about to unleash itself.

AESCHYLUS Thou cribber of Cretan monodies, inflicting on our art unholy marriages.   850

DIONYSUS Hey, Aeschylus, control yourself, your honour. Euripides, you scoundrel, you'd better get yourself out of this hailstorm, if you've any sense, so in his fury he doesn't batter your brow with his heady diction and start you spouting *Telephus*. As for you, Aeschylus, don't lose your temper. Let's   855
have a civilised debate. Wrangling's what we expect of bakers' wives, not poets. You explode into flames like an oak on fire.

EURIPIDES Well, *I* am ready – I'll not shrink from the task– to bite   860
or be bitten first, if that's what he wants, whether in my diction, my lyrics or the very fibre of my tragedies. Yes, by god. Take my *Peleus*, my *Aeolus*, my *Meleager*, even – no, especially – my *Telephus*.

DIONYSUS Aeschylus, what do you propose we do? Speak up.   865

AESCHYLUS Well, I did want to avoid an argument here. The contest between us is not on equal terms.

DIONYSUS What do you mean?

AESCHYLUS I mean that my poetry has not died with me as it has with him. He has his works with him to recite. Nevertheless, if that's what you want, that's what we must do.   870

DIONYSUS Before the contest of cleverness begins, let someone fetch incense and fire so that I can pray that my judgement will be perfectly inspired.
Chorus, sing a melody to the Muses.

Agōn: opening prayers

The contest or *agōn*, a standard component of most Greek tragedies and comedies, opens formally with prayers and the burning of incense, rituals familiar to the audience. The Chorus of Initiates call upon the nine Muses, goddesses of the arts, to observe the proceedings. Aeschylus invokes **Demeter** (886, '**Demeter**', p. 28), a choice likely to be approved by the Chorus. Euripides rejects the incense (889) and conventional gods.

882 Even the tiniest fragment or shaving The Chorus suggest that the outcome of the contest might hinge on tiny details or quibbles. This type of argument is associated particularly with the sophists, caricatured in Aristophanes' *Clouds*, with whom Euripides has much in common.

893 Air ... tongue ... wit ... nostrils The powers Euripides calls upon, like those invoked by Socrates and the Clouds (*Clouds* 264, 424), suggest a humanist perspective: e.g. tongue symbolises the power of rhetoric, unaided by the divine inspiration associated with the **Muses** (875). In *Clouds* this atheistic view of the world, at first attractive to the hero and his son, has direct moral implications that turn their world upside-down, making it right, not wrong, to beat your parents, a view emphatically rejected at the end of the play. Euripides' prayer gives the audience a hint that he may not be what Athens needs.

Agōn: prelude

As at lines 814–29, this choral song, with its metaphors of dance and war, intensifies the excitement of the contest. Again, the competitors need no names to identify them: **the one** (901) is clearly Euripides, **the other** (903) Aeschylus. Each poet responds in turn using tetrameters (four bars/line) rather than the more usual trimeter (three bars/line).

CHORUS OF INITIATES Muses, nine holy maidens of Zeus, 875
Who behold the subtle, intelligent minds
Of ingenious men, when they get in a fight
And argue their side with carefully planned
And crafty moves,
Come and observe the awesome power 880
Of these two mouths to find the right word,
Even the tiniest fragment or shaving.
Now the great contest of cleverness
Rolls into action.

DIONYSUS Say a prayer, too, each of you, before your speech. 885
AESCHYLUS Demeter, who nourishes my mind, make me worthy
of your Mysteries.
DIONYSUS You, too. Take this incense and throw it in.
EURIPIDES Thanks, but I pray to other gods.
DIONYSUS Your own personal ones? New currency? 890
EURIPIDES Very much so.
DIONYSUS Go on, then, pray to your special gods.
EURIPIDES Air, which sustains me, hinge of my tongue, native wit
and keen-scented nostrils: grant that I may grip the argument,
counter it and set him straight.

CHORUS OF INITIATES We long to hear 895
From these wise men
How their words will dance!
Begin the steps of war!
Their tongues grow fierce;
Neither lacks spirit or daring;
Their thoughts move fast.
We can doubtless expect the one 900
To pare it down to something smart,
And the other to wrench up sentences, root and all,
Attack and let loose a desert storm of words.

Agōn: Round 1 – opening remarks, Euripides (907–91)

Euripides speaks first, with the fluency of a lawyer and for a long time.
He begins by attacking the overall structure of Aeschylus' plays: the long
silences of his central characters (911–15, 919–21); the dominance of
the choral odes (914–15); the obscurity of his complex poetic language
(925–32). Dionysus agrees with his points, which are not without
substance (see 911n, 914n, **'Aeschylean language'**, p. 64).

910 Phrynichus Son of Polyphrasmon (see 1301n), he was a pioneer of
early Athenian tragedy who died in the 470s. Aeschylus, in his mid-
teens, may have seen Phrynichus celebrate his first victory *c*. 510 BC.
Aristophanes likens the poet to a bee gathering honey for his sweet
lyrics. Euripides here suggests his style was cloying.

911 Achilles or Niobe The picture below, contemporary with
Aeschylus, shows a muffled Achilles refusing to fight, resistant to
Odysseus' persuasion. Niobe is also depicted as static in art: numbed by
the deaths of her 14 children she turns to stone. Aeschylus chose these
themes for his lost plays *Myrmidons*, *Phrygians* and *Niobe*.

Red-figure cup, early 5th century BC, *from Vulci.*
Odysseus tries to persuade Achilles to return to
the fighting at Troy.

914 ode after ode In Aeschylus' *Agamemnon*, the choral *parodos* is 217
lines long. Aristotle, unlike Euripides, sets this in its historical context:
The increase in the number of actors from one to two was introduced by
Aeschylus, who cut down the role of the chorus and developed the
dialogue with actor (Poetics 4.16).

927 Alas, I am undone! Aeschylus utters the classic tragic lament,
oimoi talas.

You must each speak once you're ready. Make sure your words   905
are sophisticated, and don't use clichés or copy anyone else.

EURIPIDES OK, I will tell you about my own poetry when I get to
my closing remarks. But first, I'll cross-examine this man. I will
show that he was a charlatan and a cheat. I will demonstrate how
he deceived the audience, treating them like the ignorant fools
Phrynichus cultivated. The very first thing he'd do was sit one of   910
his characters down and cover them up – an Achilles or Niobe,
maybe – so that their face didn't show. A travesty of a tragedy!
And they'd utter not so much as a grunt.

DIONYSUS He's right. Not a grunt.

EURIPIDES And the chorus would thump out ode after ode, four in
a row. But the actors would remain silent.   915

DIONYSUS I rather liked the silences. I enjoyed them just as much
as all that wittering you get today.

EURIPIDES You were naive – you know that, of course.

DIONYSUS I agree. And what made our friend do that?

EURIPIDES It was all an act, to make the spectators sit there, just
waiting for Niobe to utter a word. The drama would go on and   920
on and on and …

DIONYSUS You utter scoundrel! So that's how I was diddled?
Why are you fidgeting and looking uncomfortable?

EURIPIDES Because I am exposing him. And, then, when he had
delivered all this rubbish and the drama was already half-way
through, he would utter a dozen words as weighty as an ox:
shaggy-crested, bushy-browed monsters, terrifying to behold.   925
Incomprehensible to the audience.

AESCHYLUS Alas, I am undone!

DIONYSUS Shut up.

Aeschylean language

Euripides parodies Aeschylus' style by piling up grandiloquent phrases, involving striking imagery and unique compound words evoking harsh landscapes, surreal creatures and war, particularly the war at Troy, where the river Scamander flows. All these elements are to be found in Aeschylus' writings and his plays are challenging for a modern reader.

932 yellow cock-horse A fragment of Aeschylus' *Myrmidons* survives in which this word describes a painted decoration on one of the Greek ships at Troy that peels off in the blaze of fire from the attack led by Hector. This episode from the *Iliad*, which leads to Achilles' beloved Patroclus entering the fight and being killed, was the subject of Aeschylus' play.

934 Eryxis It is unclear whether this minor political figure is being mocked for his appearance, sexuality or cowardice.

939 Persian tapestries Greek visual art was strongly influenced by rich oriental designs in the 7th and 6th centuries BC. The style and setting of Aeschylus' *Persians,* performed in 472 BC and set in the Persian court, would have evoked a remote past and exotic world for most of Aristophanes' audience at the end of the 5th century.

Medical diet

Euripides' regime suggests he's familiar with medical pioneers such as Hippocrates of Cos (*c*. 469–399 BC), whose innovative approach was holistic and based on scientific observation. Euripides' description of poetry's special diet is an extended metaphor, preparing us for his own simpler and more direct approach to drama.

943 the press The translation suggests both a press for making juice and printed pamphlets, books or newspapers. The Greek says 'from books'. Euripides' collection of books is mocked at 1410. Dionysus reveals a passion for reading at 53. See also 1115.

944 Cephisophon Euripides is made to acknowledge Cephisophon as collaborator on his monodies (see 860n) and adulterer in his wife's bed (see 1408), part of the complicated domestic background to which Aeschylus alludes at 947 (see also 840n).

EURIPIDES Not one word he spoke was clear...

DIONYSUS Stop grinding your teeth.

EURIPIDES ...it was all Scamandrian ditches, mattocks and
hook-beaked eagles, blazons of beaten bronze and horse-crags.
Not easy to follow.   930

DIONYSUS Goodness, yes! I once lay awake most of the night
figuring out what sort of bird a yellow cock-horse is.

AESCHYLUS It's a device emblazoned on a ship, you complete
ignoramus.

DIONYSUS And there was I thinking it was Philoxenus' son, Eryxis.

EURIPIDES And how appropriate is it anyway, to mention a cock in   935
a tragedy?

AESCHYLUS What about you, you enemy of the gods? What kind of
thing did *you* include?

EURIPIDES Unlike you, no cock-horses, by Zeus, and no goat-stags
– the sort of thing they put on Persian tapestries. When I first
took over the art from you she was obese, all swollen with   940
overweight words. The first thing I did was put her on a diet and
get that weight off with tiny extracts, exercise and baby white
beet. I got her drinking gossip straight from the press, then I
weaned her on to monodies with a little touch of Cephisophon.
After that there was no blabber of any old nonsense that popped   945
into the head, no convoluting the content. The first person on
stage would immediately explain the background.

AESCHYLUS Easier to explain than your own.

Euripidean drama: opening lines

Having accused Aeschylus of leaving his audiences confused, Euripides argues for the accessibility of his own plays, from the opening to the prologue; the surviving plays generally begin with a single character explaining the background – sometimes (*Bacchae*, *Hippolytus*) a god; sometimes a servant (*Medea*) or simple farmer (*Electra*).

952 My drama was democratic In the extract below Mozart tries to persuade the court that his new opera should be *The Marriage of Figaro*, based on Beaumarchais' play. The enthusiasm of Euripides, like that of Mozart, for the people's perspective was not popular with all – perhaps more surprising in 5th-century democratic Athens than in the French and Austrian courts just before the French Revolution.

Mozart: *Come on now, be honest! Which one of you wouldn't rather listen to his hairdresser than Hercules? Or Horatius, or Orpheus...*
people so lofty they sound as if they shit marble!
Peter Shaffer, *Amadeus*, 1979

Athenian democracy

Many late 5th- and early 4th-century Athenians did not support the democracy, as the politics of the period show (see *Background to the story*, pp. v–vii). In describing its potential dangers Plato warns of excessive liberty, where children, slaves and women are as free as their masters, *a system which treats everyone as equal whether or not they are* (*Republic* 558c, 563b). Euripides says he teaches the ordinary man to think and speak critically (953–63, 971–9) but goes further in giving women and slaves, who had almost no political status in 5th-century Athens, an equal voice (949–50). Ironically, Euripides is often charged with misogyny in Aristophanes' plays (e.g. *Thesmophoriazusae* 385–8). It is still debated whether women could attend the theatre.

953 You're not treading on the safest ground there Euripides spent his final years not in democratic Athens, but at the Macedonian court.

963 tales The stories of these heroes' deaths at Troy are not told in the *Iliad*, but are part of the cycle of Trojan myths mined by tragedians. The names of Euripides' Trojan plays give an idea of the different types of story he selected for his audience: *Iphigenia at Aulis*, *Trojan Women*, *Andromache*, *Hecuba*.

963 supporters Euripides coins two magnificent Aeschylean adjectives to characterise his rival's followers, each word 20 letters long in Greek. Despite their archaic epithets, **Phormisius** and **Megaenetus** seem to be current political figures, not voices from the past. Of Euripides' followers, both Theramenes (see 541n) and Cleitophon show dexterity as well as luck in riding the waves post-411 BC.

EURIPIDES Then, from the opening words I would let no character
remain idle. In my plays slaves and women, young and old,
would speak just as much as their masters.   950

AESCHYLUS Outrageous! You should have paid for it with your life.

EURIPIDES My drama was democratic, by Apollo.

DIONYSUS Give it a miss, old chap. You're not treading on the
safest ground there.

EURIPIDES Then I taught these people here to speak freely...

AESCHYLUS I'll say you did! Better if you'd been ripped to shreds
before giving that particular lesson.   955

EURIPIDES ...setting out subtle lines and neatly angled arguments;
how to think, to see, to understand, to twist and turn, to love
those crafty moves, stay on the lookout for trouble and keep one
step ahead.

AESCHYLUS You certainly did!

EURIPIDES I introduced domestic scenarios we can relate to and
engage with, issues inviting debate. Because they knew about it,   960
they could challenge my writing. I didn't exaggerate, dragging
them away from common sense, and I didn't dazzle them with
tales of Cycnus and Memnon and their jingling, bell-bossed
mounts. You can tell from our different supporters. His are
people like that beard-spouting-spear-clutching-trumpet-at-the-   965
ready Phormisius, and Megaenetus the Maniac, that gnasher-
flashing-bender-of-pines; whereas mine include Cleitophon and
the elegant Theramenes.

DIONYSUS Theramenes? Yes, he's a dangerously clever man in
everything he does. If he falls into trouble, or anything like it,
he's out, faster than a flick of the dice.   970

991 Meletides His name was a by-word for foolishness; he was a sort of Mr Bean of the ancient world.

Household management (975–89)

Housekeeping was the responsibility of the wife, but Xenophon's *Oeconomicus*, written not long after *Frogs*, instructs a man on how to train his wife in good household management.

- Do these outcomes of Euripides' instruction seem trivial or significant to you?

Review of Euripides' opening remarks (907–91)

- Summarise the basis of Euripides' attacks on Aeschylus and assess how much damage you think Euripides has done to his rival's reputation. How fair are his points?
- Do you think Euripides has done more good or harm to his own case? How justifiable are the claims he makes for his own superiority?
- How independent a judge does Dionysus seem to you to be (see 66)? Has he been easily manipulated by Euripides' rhetoric?
- Who do you feel is winning at this stage in the contest?

Agōn: Round 1 – opening remarks, Aeschylus (1007–98)

In a sense, Aeschylus has just enacted the role attributed by Euripides to his central characters (see 912n). He has sat silent, perhaps muffled, groaning, gnashing his teeth and making the occasional objection. The quotation from Aeschylus' *Myrmidons* (992) reinforces this impression. Dionysus and the audience now expect an incomprehensible **torrent** (1005) of **'Aeschylean language'** (see p. 64). First, though, Aeschylus asks some sharp and clear questions before going on to defend himself. He is not the unsophisticated brute Euripides has led us to expect. Aeschylus' response matches that of Euripides in length and metre (see '*Agōn*: **prelude**', p. 60).

EURIPIDES That's the kind of wisdom
I introduced to them:
Bringing questioning
And reason to my art.
So now they notice
Everything. They know what's what,   975
Like how to run their households
Better than before, keeping an eye on
How it's going, where it's gone
And who's nicked what.

DIONYSUS God, yes. Now everyone   980
In Athens gets back home
And shouts at his servants asking,
Where's that jug? Who bit off the head
Of that little sprat? That cup I got last year   985
Has gone. Where's that bit of old garlic?
And who's been nibbling the olives?
Whereas before they'd sit there, silly sods,   990
Mouths agape, like Meletides.

CHORUS OF INITIATES *You gaze upon this, glorious Achilles.*
Come, what will you say in response?
Just be careful,
And don't let that temper of yours
Take hold and whisk you off course.   995
He has made some terrible accusations.
See to it now, noble sir, that you don't
Give an angry response.
Draw in your sails, use only the edge.   1000
That way you'll bring her on little by little
Watching out for the moment to catch
A calmer, gentler breeze.

DIONYSUS Now, champion of the Greeks in towering, solemn
utterances and ornate tragic trumpery, take heart and unleash   1005
your torrent.

1010 we make better people ... better Aeschylus and Euripides seem about to engage in a Socratic dialogue. In this characteristic extract from Plato, Socrates questions what the teachings of a sophist will actually do for a young man: *Hippocrates, by becoming a pupil of Protagoras, will on the very day he joins him go home a better man, and on each successive day will make similar progress – towards what, Protagoras, and better at what?* (*Protagoras* 318d).The question, 'better at what' is unspoken, but lies behind what Aeschylus says next.

1013 Death The executions after Arginusae and death of Socrates a few years after this play are reminders that this is not pure hyperbole.

Aeschylus' defence: his characters as positive examples

Aeschylus begins, contrasting the mighty warriors in his plays with the average modern Athenian, who, he suggests, is idle and corrupt (1014–15, 1025), a view unlikely to impress the audience. Dionysus cautions him (1018) when he starts living up to Euripides' satire. Despite Dionysus' commentary, Aeschylus makes a serious point: courageous role-models can instil courage and military discipline in a citizen body.

War

The 5th century was dominated by war in Greece. The Persian invasions of 490 BC and 480–479 BC resulted in the destruction of Athens; the Peloponnesian War against Sparta and her allies lasted a whole generation and involved the regular devastation of Attica. Even between these two great wars, peace was not sustained. Athens had no professional army and each citizen would have been personally involved in the war effort, even those not well suited (see **'Rowing class'**, p. 14, and **'Pantacles'**, 1037). The virtues celebrated by Aeschylus were not marginal to Athenian life at this time.

1023 *Seven against Thebes* Set in the legendary past, the play tells how Oedipus' sons clashed in war, killing each other in single combat.

1029 Darius The Persian King Darius led the first invasion in 490 BC, resulting in his defeat at Marathon. He died in 486 BC. Aeschylus' *Persians* is set in Xerxes' reign several years later (see 939n). This may be a deliberate error to make Dionysus sound silly.

1032–5 Orpheus ... Musaeus ... Hesiod ... Homer Aeschylus' four great precedents support the argument that the poet is a teacher (1055). In myth Orpheus is famed for his attempt to rescue his wife Eurydice from death by his music; in legend he brought to Greece Egyptian practices related to the underworld and Orphic Mysteries. Musaeus, his son or disciple, was associated with the Mysteries. Hesiod (*Works and Days* is referred to here) was roughly contemporary with Homer.

AESCHYLUS I'm angry at what has happened and it makes my belly ache to have to respond to him. But so he can't claim I'm lost for words, tell me this: why should we admire a poet?

EURIPIDES For his cleverness and good advice. Because we make people in our cities better. 1010

AESCHYLUS So if you fail in this and instead turn fine, noble citizens into rogues, what would you say you deserve?

DIONYSUS Death. Don't ask him.

AESCHYLUS Now look at the sort of characters he got from me. Weren't they noble and tall – not the shirkers and layabouts, the cheats and villains you see today, but men who breathed spears 1015 and javelins, with snowy-plumed crests, helmets, greaves and hearts encased in seven layers of ox-hide?

DIONYSUS This isn't going well. Those helmets are making my head hurt.

EURIPIDES And how exactly did you teach them nobility?

DIONYSUS Go on, tell us, Aeschylus, and don't get cross or all high 1020 and mighty.

AESCHYLUS My plays were full of war.

EURIPIDES Such as?

AESCHYLUS The *Seven against Thebes*. Every man watching was filled with a passionate desire to fight.

DIONYSUS A bad move. You made the Thebans braver in battle. And for that you deserve a good beating.

AESCHYLUS And you could have been in training, but just weren't 1025 bothered. Next I directed *Persians* and taught people to yearn for a foe to defeat, glorifying this great achievement.

DIONYSUS I really liked it when the Chorus heard about Darius' death and immediately started clapping like this and saying 'Yahw-ooo-ooo'.

AESCHYLUS That's what playwrights should practise. Go back to 1030 the beginning and see how useful our noblest poets have been. Orpheus revealed the Mysteries to us and taught us not to commit murder. Musaeus gave us oracles and cures for diseases; Hesiod taught us about how to work the soil, the seasons for sowing crops and ploughing; and the divine Homer – from where does his honour and reputation derive if not from

1040 Lamachus His long military career ended when he was killed in action in the Sicilian disaster of 413 BC. In *Acharnians* (425 BC) Aristophanes ridicules his love of ostrich-feather plumes and the like in a comic arming scene and invents an adjective to reflect his obsession: 'polemolamachaicon' (1080, *polemos* means war in Greek).

1041–2 Patroclus … Teucer Each fought at Troy in the shadow of a greater warrior (Achilles and Ajax), but proved their own courage. Patroclus' heroism was depicted in *Myrmidons* (see 932n). No play by Aeschylus with Teucer as a central character survives, but he defends his half-brother's corpse from dishonour in Sophocles' *Ajax*.

Male and female virtue
If Aeschylus' male virtues seem limited to courage, patriotism and martial skill, his view of female virtue is even more restricted – to their sexual conduct. His most famous female character, Clytaemnestra in the *Oresteia*, has an adulterous affair with Aegisthus, but this is subordinate to her masculine desire for revenge.

Aeschylus' attack: Euripides' characters as negative examples
Having demonstrated the moral qualities of his characters, Aeschylus attacks first Euripidean heroines and then his male characters (1063).

1043–4 tarts like Phaedra or Stheneboea Phaedra, wife of King Theseus, falls madly in love with her step-son, Hippolytus. In Euripides' play (see 1046n) the two characters never meet on stage and the queen's determination to resist her lust leads to her suicide. Stheneboea is more culpable and is thrown to her death from the flying horse Pegasus. Her pursuit of Bellerophon leads her husband Proetus to attempt the murder of his guest. Lust concealed from their husbands makes both women **bad examples** (1053).

1046 Aphrodite Her name is used here to mean sexual love. Euripides' *Hippolytus* opens with the goddess explaining how she will punish those who reject her power. Contrary to Euripides' jibe, Aphrodite also figures in a fragment of Aeschylus' lost *Danaids*, where she speaks defending love.

1048 rebounded on you Euripides' wife was alleged to have had an affair with the poet Cephisophon (944n).

1058 human scale Euripides defends the stories he presents: as being traditional (1052) they reflect human behaviour. While he operates at the level of the kitchen sink, Aeschylus has his head in the clouds. **Lycabettos** (1056) is an impressive mountain of rock in modern Athens; **Parnassus** (1057) is the mountain that towers over Delphi.

teaching men useful things like battle order, courage and 1035
weaponry?

DIONYSUS He didn't manage to teach Pantacles, that cack-handed idiot! The other day in the procession he was trying to fasten his crest after he'd put his helmet on!

AESCHYLUS But he did teach many other fine men, including the legendary Lamachus. My inspiration, modelled on his, has 1040 created many examples of virtue – like Patroclus and the lion-hearted Teucer – so that I could stir any citizen to emulate such men when he hears the trumpet call. And, by Zeus, my creations do not include tarts like Phaedra or Stheneboea. No. No one can say there's anything erotic in the women I have created.

EURIPIDES God, no, not a hint of sex from you. 1045

AESCHYLUS I should hope not. Whereas Aphrodite laid full-on siege to you and your plays. She was your downfall.

DIONYSUS That's right, by Zeus. What you wrote about other men's wives rebounded on you.

EURIPIDES And what harm did my Stheneboeas ever do to the city, you old fool?

AESCHYLUS You persuaded noble ladies, wives of noble husbands, 1050 to drink hemlock because they were ashamed of your Bellerophon.

EURIPIDES Did I invent a story about Phaedra that wasn't there already?

AESCHYLUS Of course not, but a poet should keep bad examples hidden, not parade them or use them to teach. Children have teachers to instruct them, young men have poets. We have an 1055 obligation to speak what's good.

EURIPIDES So if you speak with the grandeur of Mount Lycabettos or Parnassus, does that teach us what's good? Shouldn't you communicate on a human scale?

AESCHYLUS You wretched creature, great thoughts and ideas must bring forth words of a similar scale. Besides, demi-gods must be 1060 expected to speak on a higher level, just as they dress more magnificently than us. You degraded all the fine things I introduced.

1063 kings in rags Similar generalised accusations have already been made (841, 846). In addition to the example of Telephus (855n), Orestes appears in disguise in *Iphigenia in Tauris* and Menelaus in *Helen*. Ragged or crippled kings are also found in Homer's *Odyssey* and Sophocles' *Philoctetes*. Aeschylus argues that disguising responsibility produces hypocrites (1066), layabouts (1070) and general insubordination (1071–3). Dionysus is quick to recognise the symptoms and elaborate.

1071 *Paralus* One of two elite triremes, manned by Athenian citizens and sent on special state missions. Triremes were fast warships with three banks of oars, each one set slightly above the other, hence the farting joke (1074). The crew of this ship were known as extreme democrats.

1083 as a result Even if Aeschylus is right that Athens has more than its share of undesirable bureaucrats and **mob-monkeys** (1085) (demagogues, see 569–70n), can he prove a causal connection? The scandals in Euripides' plays from which he generalises include Phaedra's nurse, who secretly approaches Hippolytus on her mistress's behalf (**pimps**, 1080), the birth of Telephus in Athena's temple, and the incest of Aeolus' children, also found in Homer's *Odyssey* 10. The context of the sophistic aphorism 'life is not living' (1082) (see also 1477) is unknown.

Torch-race
On the fifth night of the Panathenaea a torch-race was held with teams of runners competing in relay along the 2½ km course. They ran from the Academy to the temple of Athena on the Acropolis, passing into the city through the Dipylon gate in the Ceramicus and on to the Agora (see plan, p. x). Other ritual torch-races took place, sometimes on horse-back (Plato, *Republic* 328a). Lack of fitness results from spending time sitting in the agora instead of going to the gym (see also 1069–70). The same problem with 'young people today' is voiced in *Clouds* (1002–3).

Late 5th-century Panathenaic vase showing an athlete running with a torch.

EURIPIDES By doing what?

AESCHYLUS First of all, you dressed kings in rags to make them
seem pitiable to people.

EURIPIDES And where's the harm in doing that?

AESCHYLUS That's the reason no one wealthy is willing to fund a   1065
trireme; instead they wrap themselves in rags and weep,
claiming to be poor.

DIONYSUS While underneath they've got a nice, woolly fleece, by
Demeter. And then, if they get away with their lies, up they pop
at the fish counter.

AESCHYLUS Secondly, you taught people to waste time in idle
chatter and gossip. It's emptied the gyms. Our young men sit
around gossiping, wearing their buttocks out. It's encouraged the   1070
crew of the *Paralus* to answer back to their superiors; when I was
alive all they knew was how to ask for a biscuit and shout
'Heave-ho!'

DIONYSUS – and how to fart in the face of the rower below, cover
their messmates in shit and nick a change of clothes ashore.   1075
These days they answer back and won't row any more; they just
sail off wherever they like.

AESCHYLUS What troubles can we *not* blame him for?
           Isn't *he* the man who put on public show
               Pimps, women giving birth in temples,   1080
           Girls having sex with their brothers and
                Claiming that life is not living?
            And as a result our city's been filled
         With petty clerks and thieving mob-monkeys   1085
              Who constantly rip the people off.
            No one can carry a torch these days
                 Because they're so unfit.

DIONYSUS   You're right, they can't.
           I nearly died laughing at the Panathenaea: 1090
     This man was running slowly, head down, pale, fat,
    Way behind and really struggling. As he reached the
            Ceramicus gate, the locals whacked him
                  In the stomach, ribs,   1095

Review of Aeschylus' opening remarks (1007–98)

- Do you accept Aeschylus' principle that our behaviour is influenced, for better or worse, by the role-models we see on stage or screen?
- Have you become more or less supportive of Aeschylus by line 1088? What are your reasons?
- Do you think, from his remarks since 907, that Dionysus has proved himself a suitable judge of this contest?
- Read lines 1099–1118. Can you detect any favouritism from the Chorus in these lines towards either of the contestants?

1118 smart Flattering the audience's intelligence was a wise move for a comic poet. The mention of books suggests growing levels of literacy and connects the audience with Euripides (53n, 943n, 1410).

Agōn: Round 2, part i: Euripides attacks Aeschylus' prologues
Euripides begins with the claim that Aeschylus' prologues (unlike his own – see p. 66) fail to set out the story clearly (1121). He selects two of the **number** of criticisms (1123) he loftily claims he could make. The nit-picking approach we see in these lines is a style associated with the sophists (see 882n). Such arguments appear clever, but often defy common sense.

1119 prologues This is the technical term used of Greek comedy and tragedy to refer to the opening section of the play before the *parodos* (arrival of the Chorus – see p. 24). The prologue of *Frogs* therefore ends at line 312 (but see **'Chorus'**, p. 16).

1124 *Oresteia* Euripides begins with an attack on Aeschylus' most celebrated work. This trilogy (458 BC) comprised *Agamemnon*, *Choephoroi* (*Libation-bearers*) and *Eumenides*. Lines 1126–7 are from an earlier version of *Choephoroi*. (See **'Orestes'**, p. 78.)

Sides and buttocks,
And as they were smacking him
He let out an almighty fart,
Blew out the torch, and fled!

CHORUS OF INITIATES A weighty matter, mighty conflict,
Violent clash is on us.   1100
It's hard to make a choice.
When one has made a forceful point,
The other spins it back
And fiercely stands his ground.   1105
So, you two, don't just sit there.
There are plenty more clever attacks to be made.
Whatever challenge either can offer, speak out,
Attack, strip back the layers, ancient and modern.
Take a risk: say something smart and subtle.   1110
If what alarms you is the ignorance
Of the audience, the fear they may not see
The subtlety of your arguments, don't panic.
It's not like that any more. They've all seen combat;
They've got the book and grasped the finer points.   1115
Born with natural talent, now they're razor sharp.
So don't be nervous, come on out and face them,
For the audience, at any rate, is smart.

EURIPIDES Right, I shall turn to those prologues of yours, so that
my very first test is of the opening sections of this *brilliant*   1120
tragedian. You see, his exposition of the story lacked clarity.

DIONYSUS How are you going to test this?

EURIPIDES A number of ways. First, recite to me a prologue from
your *Oresteia*.

DIONYSUS Right. Be quiet, everyone. Speak, Aeschylus.   1125

AESCHYLUS *Earth-born Hermes, watching over a father's realm,*
Be my saviour and ally, I beseech you,
For I have come to this land and returned.

DIONYSUS What can you find fault with in that?

EURIPIDES Oh, only a dozen things.

DIONYSUS But that's only three lines in total.   1130

1131 twenty An example of comic hyperbole. The number of alleged errors per line has increased dramatically since line 1129; **keep quiet** (1132) suggests that Aeschylus is finding all this hard to take.

1136 See? What nonsense! The manuscripts do not indicate who is speaking. All three characters have been proposed for this line.
- Which character do you think this line suits best?

1139 *a father's realm* Orestes speaks these lines. Euripides exploits a lack of clarity as to whose realm Orestes means. Euripides takes it to be that of Orestes' father (Agamemnon), and argues that *no* god can possibly have been ***watching over*** (1126) it, given Agamemnon's brutal death on his return from Troy; this is the **immediate error** (1135). Aeschylus explains that Hermes was not watching over Orestes' father's realm (Argos), but the realm of the dead, where Agamemnon was. Hermes played the important role of escorting souls to the underworld (his **chthonic role**, 1147). This still leaves problems because Hermes was the son of Zeus, not of Hades, lord of the dead, but Euripides seems unconcerned about this **mistake** (1148).

1149 rob tombs Euripides begins a smart response (1147), but we never hear it in full because Dionysus butts in, connecting Hermes, god of the dead (**Eriounios**, 1146) with Hermes, god of thieves. Hermes was also messenger to the gods and patron of merchants and of travellers, an appropriate god for the returning Orestes to invoke.

1150 sour grapes Aeschylus shows resentment that the god of wine is siding with his opponent. It doesn't stop Dionysus (see 1158–9).

1153 *come to this land and returned* Euripides criticises Aeschylus' use of synonyms, a feature of elevated poetic and rhetorical style, arguing that the second expression adds nothing to the sense. Rather surprisingly, Aeschylus defends himself using his opponent's sophistic, hair-splitting technique (1166).

1159 a dish, or rather a bowl In Greek both words mean a 'kneading trough', used for making bread. Dionysus contributes to the debate, introducing a banal, domestic example that the audience may have heard before: the comic poet Pherecrates uses the same example.

Orestes

Orestes was taken away from Argos/Mycenae at a very young age when it was clear that his life was in danger from Aegisthus. He returned secretly on reaching adulthood to take vengeance. The story of his return, reunion with his sister Electra and murder of their mother Clytaemnestra and her lover Aegisthus inspired many plays. Versions by each of the three tragedians survive.

EURIPIDES And each one contains twenty mistakes.

DIONYSUS Aeschylus, I suggest you keep quiet. If not, you'll be
paying for more than just the three lines.

AESCHYLUS You want *me* to be quiet for *him*?

DIONYSUS Yes, that's my advice.

EURIPIDES He made an immediate error, one that cries out to the   1135
heavens.

AESCHYLUS See? What nonsense! But it really doesn't bother me.
What do you mean, 'error'?

EURIPIDES Say it again, from the beginning.

AESCHYLUS *Earth-born Hermes, watching over a father's realm...*

EURIPIDES Didn't Orestes say this at the tomb of his dead father?   1140

AESCHYLUS He did.

EURIPIDES Then did he claim that Hermes was *watching over* his
father, when he died violently at the hands of his own wife and
by means of a stealthy trick?

AESCHYLUS That's not what he meant. He was calling on Hermes-   1145
Eriounios, as he made clear by mentioning that he'd taken on the
chthonic role from his father.

EURIPIDES Then your mistake is even worse than I thought. If the
chthonic honour was his father's –

DIONYSUS – then Hermes learned to rob tombs from his dad.

AESCHYLUS Dionysus, those are sour grapes you're drinking.   1150

DIONYSUS Try another line. And you, watch out for any faults.

AESCHYLUS *Be my saviour and ally I beseech you,*
For I have come to this land and returned.

EURIPIDES The brilliant Aeschylus has told us the same thing
twice.

DIONYSUS What do you mean, twice?   1155

EURIPIDES Consider what he said. Let me explain:
He says, 'I have come to this land and returned', but 'I have come'
is the same thing as 'I returned.'

DIONYSUS So it is, by Zeus. Just like someone saying to his
neighbour, 'Lend me a dish, or rather a bowl.'

AESCHYLUS These things are not the same, you pumped-up   1160
windbag. They are an excellent choice of words.

1167–9 That's good, by Apollo/Hermes For once Dionysus is impressed by both poets. The distinctions between *come* and *return* explained here (1164–6) seem slippery and unconvincing. Aristophanes is parodying a sophistic style of argument – and exposing the naivety of those who, like Dionysus, are taken in by it.

1173 *to hear, to listen* Aeschylus seems to walk into Euripides' trap, but Dionysus springs to the older poet's defence.

1176 the third go The three-fold address is found in Homer, for example when Odysseus' crew mourn their dead comrades, killed by the Cicones: *I did not let my curved ships set sail before calling on my wretched companions three times* (*Odyssey* 10.65). The idea remains a feature of epic poetry. Aeneas, e.g., tries three times to embrace the ghost of his dead wife (*Aeneid* 2.792).

1179 spit on me Euripides' confidence as he enters this stage of the duel is clear; the words **extraneous padding** remind the audience of his previous claims of a new, slim-line approach to drama (see 940–7).

DIONYSUS How? Explain what you mean.

AESCHYLUS To 'come' to a land works well for anyone with a
homeland – he has simply 'come' without mishap. But a man   1165
who is in exile has both 'come' and 'returned'.

DIONYSUS That's good, by Apollo. What do you say, Euripides?

EURIPIDES I say that Orestes did not make a 'return' home. He
came back secretly, without the authorities' consent.

DIONYSUS That's good, by Hermes; although I don't understand a
word you're saying.

EURIPIDES Then carry on. Try another line.

DIONYSUS Get on with it, then, Aeschylus. Hurry up.   1170
And you, look out for anything dodgy.

AESCHYLUS *And on this burial mound, I cry out to my father*
to hear, to listen.

EURIPIDES There it is again – he said the same thing twice, quite
clearly, *to hear, to listen.*

DIONYSUS Well, he was talking to the dead, my poor fellow. You   1175
can't get through to them even on the third go.
Anyway, how did you start your prologues?

EURIPIDES I'll tell you: and if I say the same thing twice or if you
see any extraneous padding, spit on me.

DIONYSUS Go on, then, speak. I simply must hear these perfectly   1180
turned prologues of yours.

Agōn: Round 2, part ii: Aeschylus attacks Euripides' prologues

Euripides is not able to complete one line before Aeschylus begins his attack. Although he starts by picking holes in Euripides' choice of individual words, he quickly changes tack and ends up ridiculing his rival's poetry with a simple but devastating prop (1201n, 1223n).

1183 Oedipus The Theban king's name means **swollen** foot (1193) and Aeschylus summarises his story (1190–6), known to many modern audiences from Sophocles' version and much admired by Aristotle. Sophocles' play opens with Oedipus at the height of his prosperity and shows, using suspense and dramatic irony, how he learns the truth of his misfortune. Euripides' opening is more direct. Aeschylus' argument that Oedipus was never **lucky** (1183) resembles the lesson Solon teaches Croesus (Herodotus 1.32), that no man should be called lucky until he's dead. Many tragedies, including Sophocles' *Oedipus*, end with the Chorus speaking these words. Unlike the Croesus story, Oedipus' tragedy has already taken place; he has only to discover it.

1196 Erasinides One of the eight generals prosecuted in the assembly at Athens after the victory at Arginusae (see *Background to the story*, pp. v–vii).

1201 little bottle of olive oil The Greek, *lekythion*, is a small *lekythos* (illustration, p. 16), a flask used for olive oil and at funerals; the smaller version may have held more precious perfume and was handy for trips to the baths (1223n). Some scholars see sexual innuendo, hinted at in this translation at 1215, but the humour in this part of the *agōn* lies chiefly in the bathetic effect of this small household object deflating the tragedian through the repetition of a joke which works well because an audience, clever or not (see 1118), can see it coming. The Greek also makes Euripides' use of metre look too predictable.

1208 Aegyptus In Aeschylus' play *The Suppliants*, Danaus settles in Argos with his 50 daughters (the Danaids) but is pursued by his jealous twin brother Aegyptus and his 50 sons, who intend marriage. On their father's orders, all the girls except one murder their new husbands on their wedding night. Euripides' version does not survive.

1212 Dionysus This is the image of Dionysus familiar from Euripides' *Bacchae* (67n, 486n) and from Greek art (see illustration, p. 40), the god who inspires his followers to follow him into the mountains in ecstatic worship, dancing dressed in fawnskins and carrying thyrsi, fennel wands decorated with ivy. (For **Parnassus**, see 1057.)

1217 no man...is blessed in everything The opening of Euripides' *Stheneboea* (see 1043–4n) contains another important Greek precept (see 1183n), found in Homer (*Iliad* 24.527–33) and tragedies such as *Oedipus*.

EURIPIDES *Oedipus was at first a lucky man...*

AESCHYLUS No, he wasn't, by Zeus. Misfortune was in his nature. Before he was born or even existed, Apollo said he would kill his   1185 father. So how was he *at first a lucky man*?

EURIPIDES *He then became in turn of all men the most wretched.*

AESCHYLUS No, he didn't, by Zeus. Became? He never stopped! And how? When he was first born it was winter and they put   1190 him out in a pot so he would not grow up to become his father's murderer. Then he limped off to Polybus on his swollen feet. Next he married an old woman, even though he was still a youth, and, what's more, she was his own mother. Then he   1195 blinded himself.

DIONYSUS Well, he was lucky up to a point. He could have held command with Erasinides.

EURIPIDES You're talking nonsense. My prologues are well written.

AESCHYLUS By god, I'm not going to pick away at your expressions word by word. With the help of the gods – and with a little bottle   1200 of olive oil – I will destroy your prologues.

EURIPIDES With a little bottle? You – destroy my prologues?

AESCHYLUS Yes, just one. You write in such a way that one fits all with your iambics – a little blanket, a little bottle, a little baggage. I'll show you right now.

EURIPIDES Oh, you will, will you?   1205

AESCHYLUS I will.

EURIPIDES I'd better give you a line, then.
Aegyptus, so the story often goes, sailed with his fifty sons to Argos,
Where he...

AESCHYLUS *... lost his little bottle.*

DIONYSUS What little bottle? Won't he be upset?   1210
Give us another prologue so that I can see again.

EURIPIDES *Dionysus, dressed in fawnskin, armed with thyrsus,*
Leapt and danced amid the torches on Parnassus and...

AESCHYLUS *... lost his little bottle.*

DIONYSUS Oh dear. A direct hit from the bottle again.

EURIPIDES It's no problem. He won't be able to insert a bottle of oil   1215 into this prologue.
There's no man who is blessed in everything.

1222 You should trim your sails Greek tragedians often use seafaring metaphors. When winds are strong, a ship is at risk unless it reduces its sails. Dionysus jokes that the little bottle is a big threat.

1223 knock that thing out of his hand Does Aeschylus actually have a stage prop? The text gives opportunities for physical humour. Dionysus certainly gives the impression that he's talking about a real bottle, but his credulity is part of the humour. Euripides or Dionysus would seem more likely than Aeschylus to be carrying a *lekythion*, given what we learn of attitudes to baths in *Clouds* 1045–6.

Myths and opening lines
The audience, educated by years of festivals, might have enjoyed identifying the play or the myth referred to.

1225 *Cadmus* Originally from Sidon in Phoenicia, he was sent by his father ***Agenor*** in search of his lost sister Europa. Cadmus came to Thebes, where he founded a city and sowed a dragon's teeth which grew into men, in accordance with the command of the Delphic oracle.

1232 *Tantalus* To test the omniscience of the gods, he cut up his son ***Pelops*** and served him to the gods in a stew. He failed to trick the other gods, but Demeter, grieving for her lost daughter Persephone, absent-mindedly ate Pelops' shoulder. The gods restored him to life and gave him a prosthetic shoulder made of ivory. Pelops went on to win the hand of Hippodamia in marriage by beating her father in a chariot race. The lines are from the opening of Euripides' *Iphigenia in Tauris*.

1240 *Oeneus* The king of Calydon's troubles started when he sacrificed to the gods but inadvertently missed out Artemis. She sent a great boar which ravaged the land. Heroes from all over Greece gathered to hunt it and it was finally killed by Atalanta and Meleager. These lines are from *Meleager*.

Either nobly born, he's lost the means to live
Or else, ill-starred, he's ...

AESCHYLUS *...lost his little bottle.*

DIONYSUS Euripides. 1220

EURIPIDES What is it?

DIONYSUS You should trim your sails. There's a lot of puff left in that little bottle.

EURIPIDES I wouldn't think of it, by Demeter. This one will knock that thing out of his hand.

DIONYSUS Go on, then, give us another, and mind out for that bottle of oil.

EURIPIDES *The towers of Sidon Cadmus, son of Agenor,* 1225
Had barely left behind when suddenly he ...

AESCHYLUS *...lost his little bottle.*

DIONYSUS Oh dear, poor you. Just buy the bottle so that he can't demolish our prologues.

EURIPIDES What? Pay him?

DIONYSUS If you take my advice.

EURIPIDES Absolutely not. I still have plenty of prologues to recite, 1230
And he won't be able to stick his bottle in any of them.
Pelops, son of Tantalus, on his way to Pisa
With horses swift ...

AESCHYLUS *...lost his little bottle.*

DIONYSUS You see, once again, he's applied the bottle of oil.
My dear chap, just buy it now. It'll only cost you an obol, and it's 1235
very good quality.

EURIPIDES By Zeus, not yet. I have many more.
Once Oeneus from his land set out and ...

AESCHYLUS *...lost his little bottle.*

EURIPIDES Allow me first to recite the whole verse.
Once Oeneus from his land set out 1240
With corn in plenty for his sacrifice,
And in the act of honouring the gods,
He ...

AESCHYLUS *...lost his little bottle.*

DIONYSUS While he was sacrificing? Who took it from him this time?

1244 *Zeus, who has been spoken of in truth* The line is from a lost play, *Melanippe*. As the humiliation of Euripides gathers pace, Aeschylus interrupts more quickly, after a single line.

Review of Round 2

- At the end of Round 2, do you think Dionysus' sympathies have shifted? If so, when and why?

Agōn: Round 3 – lyric passages

So far, the poets have been criticising each other's spoken lines (*iambics*) only. In this round, they turn their attention to lyric poetry (860n). This verse, more poetic and elusive in content, was accompanied by music and resembled a modern opera rather than a play. The poets appear to know each other's work well and several lines from surviving plays can be identified (1264n, 1285n).

Euripides begins (1261–78) by parodying the predictable content and style of Aeschylus' choral odes, where the chorus sang accompanied by an *aulos*. This instrument, often translated as 'flute' rather than **pipes** (313), looked like two oboes joined together (see p. 88) and sounded like bagpipes without the drones. After this Euripides parodies more choral lyrics (1285–95), this time to the imaginary accompaniment of a cithara (1282n). Aeschylus then goes on the offensive, choosing a crude accompaniment for Euripides' choral lyrics (1309–23); finally in this round, he gives an outrageous performance of a Euripidean monody (1331–64).

1259 Bacchic king Aeschylus is honoured in this phrase as a master of Dionysus' art of theatre.

1263 pebbles Dionysus again seems childish as he adopts the role of score-keeper – with a short concentration span (1279–80).

1264 *Phthian Achilles* The first two lines are from Aeschylus' *Myrmidons*, where the chorus appeal to Achilles to defend the Greeks from Hector's attack (see 933n). In subsequent quotations, Euripides tacks the same second line on again, demonstrating metrical monotony. The translation tries to achieve this by rhyming with *nigh* (1265 etc.).

1268 That's two blows Part of the humour in this round of the contest comes from the literal interpretation Dionysus puts on the verse.

1273 *bee-guardians* A term for the priestesses who served in the temple of Artemis at Ephesus, and other goddesses – notably Hecate.

EURIPIDES You, keep out of it. Let's see what he has to say to this:
Zeus, who has been spoken of in truth, has…

DIONYSUS You're killing me! He'll say, *lost his little bottle.*   1245
This little bottle pops up in your prologues like a stye in the eye.

So what about his lyric passages?

EURIPIDES I have ways of showing that he is a bad lyric poet and
always writes the same things.   1250

CHORUS OF INITIATES How will this affair turn out?
I can't imagine how he'll fault
The author of by far
The best and greatest lyrics   1255
Of anybody yet.
I wonder how he'll criticise
This Bacchic king.
I fear for him.   1260

EURIPIDES His lyric passages certainly are remarkable, you'll soon
see. For I will reduce all his lyrics to one.

DIONYSUS I'll get some pebbles and keep count.

EURIPIDES *Phthian Achilles, why on hearing war's death-cry –*
Ayee the blow, come you not nigh to the rescue?   1265
Lake-dwellers, let us show our respect:
Hermes, we your race from years gone by,
Ayee the blow, come you not nigh to the rescue?

DIONYSUS That's two blows, Aeschylus.

EURIPIDES *Greece's glory, child of Atreus,*
Learn from me, o ruler high –   1270
Ayee the blow, come you not nigh to the rescue?

DIONYSUS That's the third blow, Aeschylus.

EURIPIDES *Hush, here at the shrine of Artemis the bee-guardians*
Attend, and will open it by and by –
Ayee the blow, come you not nigh to the rescue?   1275
Mine's the power to sing and sigh

1282 accompanied by the cithara The cithara was a string instrument used by rhapsodes (professional performers) to accompany Homeric verse, not Aeschylean choruses, so this is a travesty. It was held in the crook of the arm and plucked by the fingers or with a plectrum, like the smaller lyre which used a tortoise-shell as the body of the instrument. The more strongly built cithara had better projection and suited the demands of a large public audience.

1286 *Phlatto-thratto-phlatto-thrat* This onomatopoeic effect of plosive 'p's and 't's (pronounced 'puh'/'tuh') crudely imitates the strumming of a cithara. The repetition undermines the adulterated verses from *Agamemnon* below (107–10), making them feel ponderous and disconnected.

> *The twin-throned majesty of the Achaeans,*
> *Like-minded leaders of Hellas' youth,*
> *Are sped on their way by a bird-omen against the land of Teucer,*
> *Hands of vengeance on their spears:* (trans. De May)

Piper and dancer with castanets. Interior of red-figure cup by Epictetus. Boston.

1298 Marathon The site of the first great Athenian victory of the Persian Wars in 490 BC. While disparaging him, Dionysus reminds his audience that Aeschylus fought in the battle, where his brother lost his hand and his life (Herodotus 6.114).

1301 Phrynichus (see 910n) Aeschylus is claiming originality for his work and follows it up with an attack on Euripides for being derivative and using low-brow sources.

1306 Muse of Euripides From what we have just heard of Euripides' sources, it is not hard to imagine how the non-speaking actor, a masked youth, might appear and dance, to the accompaniment of castanets (see illustration above) to Aeschylus' pastiche of Euripides' choral lyrics (1309–22).

> *As fateful troops of men pass by –*
> *Ayee the blow, come you not nigh to the rescue?*

DIONYSUS …King Zeus – that's a lot of blows! I need to go to the
bathroom. All those blows have ballooned my bladder. 1280

EURIPIDES Not until you've heard his next collection of songs
written to be accompanied by the cithara.

DIONYSUS All right, go ahead, but no more blows.

EURIPIDES *The twin-throned power, the youth of Greece,* 1285
> *Phlatto-thratto-phlatto-thrat,*
> *Sent the queen-bitch, ill-starred Sphinx,*
> *Phlatto-thratto-phlatto-thrat,*
> *A violent bird with vengeful claw and spear,*
> *Phlatto-thratto-phlatto-thrat,* 1290
> *Granted the eager, aerial hounds,*
> *Phlatto-thratto-phlatto-thrat,*
> *To swoop on Ajax from the air,*
> *Phlatto-thratto-phlatto-thrat.* 1295

DIONYSUS What is all this 'phlatto-thrat'? Some song you picked
up at Marathon or from some well-attendant?

AESCHYLUS No. I took them from a fine source for a good cause,
to avoid being seen harvesting the same sacred meadow of the 1300
Muses as Phrynichus. *He* on the other hand borrows anything
from brothel ballads to romantic love songs, traditional and
exotic, dirges and dances. You'll see in a minute. Someone get
me a lyre.

But what do we need a lyre for? Where's that girl who clicks the 1305
castanets? Come over here, Muse of Euripides. Now she's the
kind of accompaniment required.

DIONYSUS This Muse never performed in Lesbian mode. No way.

AESCHYLUS *Halcyons, who coo*
> *Beside the restless* 1310
> *Waves of the sea,*
> *Your skin moist,*
> *Bedewed with wing-drops;*
>
> *And you, under the eves,*
> *In the corners,*

1308 Lesbian The modern word for a female homosexual is taken from the 6th-century BC poetess Sappho who lived on the island of Lesbos. In 5th-century Greece, Lesbos was still famed as a centre of poetical excellence and sexual 'inventiveness' (Dover), *Greek Homosexuality*.

1315 *spi-i-i-i-in* Aeschylus parodies the mode of delivery by drawing out the vowel on the word 'spin' into a long melisma. The Greek *hei-ei-ei-ei-ei-ei-liss-et-e* is used again in a shorter form at 1350.

● Consider ways of performing this ode – the mode of delivery, music, choreography and appearance of the Muse. Does it support Aeschylus' case? Do you find it funny, embarrassing or cute?

1323 Did you notice that foot? A foot is a measure of time in Greek metre, like a bar of music, leaving the potential for word-play. Aeschylus and Dionysus continue to sing as they discuss the foot, referring to Euripides' technical ability as well as to a trip, perhaps, or pretty foot on stage.

1328 certain tart The Greek names her as Cyrene, a famous and versatile *hetaira* (courtesan).

1330 solos Aeschylus now turns to monody (see 860n), an extended solo sung by a main character which is usually reserved for moments of high emotion. No context is offered (or likely) for this monody.

Tragic?
The lament in 1331–63 tells a story: a woman wakes from a frightening dream. She tries to avert it, but discovers it is true; after reflecting on how it happened, she seeks revenge and restitution. The crime she is victim to is the theft of her cockerel. The humour comes from the incongruity of the elevated emotional language and music compared with the everyday subject-matter. Aeschylus' implicit point is that a personal tragedy of this nature is not a public tragedy.

● Do you agree?

1339 *water from the river* River- or sea-water was the preferred source for ritual washing of pollution – here caused by the nightmare. The seriousness is undermined by instructions to the maids to warm up the water – a domestic touch, out of keeping with the horror – followed by the grand invocation to Poseidon (***god of the sea***, 1342). There is more bathos when we discover that in response to the loss of a small domestic animal, divine Nymphs are disturbed in their mountain dwellings.

1343 *Glyce* The name of the maid means something like 'sweetie'.

Long-fingered spiders, who
Spi-i-i-i-in your thread on the loom,   1315
In time to the singing-shuttle;

Where the pipe-loving dolphin
Leaps round dark-pointed prows,
Oracle and racetracks,
The sparkle of wine-flowered bunches of grapes,   1320
The toil-ending cluster.
Fling your arms around me, child!
Did you notice that foot?

EURIPIDES   Yes.
AESCHYLUS   And? What about you?
DIONYSUS   I did.
AESCHYLUS   That's the sort of stuff you wrote;   1325
                  You dare criticise *my* lyric poetry
                  While using yourself the same
                  Twelve tricks. As a certain tart.

So much for your lyric songs. Now I want to analyse the style of
your solos.   1330

O gloom of dark-shining night,
What ill-fated dream do you send me,
Forth from unseen Hades,
With lifeless life,
Child of black Night, shudder-inducing, terrible sight, 1335
Dark-dressed-death,
The stare of bloodshed, bloodshed,
And grip of mighty claws?

Maids, light the lamp for me, draw
Water from the river in jugs and warm it that I may wash off this
divine vision.   1340
Oh, god of the sea, so that's it.
Ah, house-mates, behold the signs:
My cockerel has been stolen.
Glyce's taken him, off and away.

1353 *grief, grief, tears, tears* Aeschylus mercilessly parodies Euripides' use of duplication for effect in his choral odes.

1356 *Cretans* The Cretans, known as excellent archers, are summoned as crack forces for this difficult and important task. The audience are possibly being reminded of Euripides' play *Cretans*. **Ida** is the mountain on Crete where Zeus was first reared.

1359 *Dictynna* A Cretan Nymph who was one of Artemis' companions in the hunt, but the name ('Netter') frequently refers to Artemis herself, goddess of hunting.

1362 *ransack* The term used in Greek is a precise Athenian legal term for searching for stolen property thought to be hidden in a house.

1363 *Hecate* A chthonic (underworld) goddess, invoked in dark magic and witchcraft. She is also sometimes identified with Artemis.

Review of Round 3
- Which poet do you think wins Round 3 (see p. 86)?
- Why do you think Dionysus stops the singing at line 1364?

Agōn: Round 4 – the scales (1364–1411)
As anticipated earlier, the scales are now introduced (797n) at the request of Aeschylus. Unlike the Egyptian Scales of the Dead, setting the soul against the feather of Truth, this contest is comically mercantile: rather than proving **worth** (1366), they reflect sheer weight, quantity with no reference to quality.

Mountain-dwelling Nymph,
Mania, catch her! 1345

I, poor wretch,
Was going about my tasks,
The spindle's centre
Spi-i-i-i-ning in my hands
Making wool, so I could get to market 1350
Before dawn and sell my wares.
But up he flew, up he flew into the sky
On the nimblest wing-tips. 1355
And left me grief, grief,
Tears, tears from my eyes
Pouring forth, pouring forth in my misery.

Cretans, children of Ida, grab your bows
And come to my aid, leap into action,
Surround the building.
And with you, let Dictynna, lovely maid,
And her pack of young hounds
Run free through the house. 1360

Daughter of Zeus, lifting in your hands
The bright-lit double-flamed torches; Hecate,
Light up the way to Glyce's house
So I can go and ransack the place.

DIONYSUS Both of you, stop that singing now!

AESCHYLUS Yes, I've had quite enough of that. I'd like to take him over to the scales. These alone can test our poetry. The weight of 1365 our phrases will prove our worth.

DIONYSUS Come over here, then, if I really must weigh up the skill of poets as if I were selling cheese.

CHORUS OF INITIATES It's not easy being clever. 1370
Here's another marvel,
Novel and full of surprise.
Could anyone else have thought this up?
If I hadn't heard it here 1375

Surprise

Costumes, scenery and props in the festivals of Dionysus could be elaborate, a way of reflecting the sponsor's wealth and generosity (95n). Round 4 might be a good moment in the play to delight the audience with **another marvel** (1371) on stage – the great balance that will weigh the poetry, perhaps the *mēchanē*, a crane designed to fly in gods to bring closure at the end of a tragedy.

- Do you think a set of scales (or equivalent) on stage would enhance or detract from the action of lines 1364–1411?
- Consider what (if anything) you might use to represent the scales in a modern production.
- How much difference does it make to the feel of a production if the chorus or audience are vocal in their support of one or other candidate?

First attempt

Euripides' line (1382) is the famous opening to his *Medea*, when the nurse wishes 'If only ...'. This is a weighty thought, wishing history could be written again. Aeschylus wins, however, with a landscape. ***Spercheius*** (1383) is a river in Malis where Philoctetes came from.

Second attempt

Each poet goes for an abstract concept in the next round. ***Persuasion*** (1391), the purpose of rhetoric, characterises Euripides as sophistic. Dionysus utters his first weighty remark for some time, that Persuasion has no substance: you can persuade someone of anything. The quotations come from Aeschylus' *Niobe* and a lost *Antigone* by Euripides.

I'd not have believed it.
I'd have suspected someone
Was talking bollocks.

DIONYSUS Come on, then. You two, stand beside the scales.

AESCHYLUS+EURIPIDES Ready.

DIONYSUS Each of you, select a line and deliver it.

Don't let go until I say 'cock-a-doodle-doo'. 1380

AESCHYLUS+EURIPIDES Got one.

DIONYSUS Each say your line into the pan.

EURIPIDES *If only the ship Argo had not flown on her winged way.*

AESCHYLUS *River Spercheius, and haunts of grazing herds.*

DIONYSUS Cock-a-doodle-doo.

AESCHYLUS+EURIPIDES Let go.

DIONYSUS This one is dropping much lower than the other. 1385

EURIPIDES Why's that?

DIONYSUS Because he put a river in, and soaked the line, just like wool-sellers do when they sell wool. Whereas your words had wings.

AESCHYLUS Get him to say another line and weigh it against mine.

DIONYSUS OK. Choose again. 1390

AESCHYLUS+EURIPIDES Ready!

DIONYSUS Speak.

EURIPIDES *Persuasion has no temple other than reason.*

AESCHYLUS *Alone of all the gods, Death desires not gifts.*

DIONYSUS Let go.

AESCHYLUS+EURIPIDES OK.

DIONYSUS Aeschylus' pan is going down again. That's because he put in Death, the weightiest of evils.

EURIPIDES Yes, but I put in Persuasion, a champion word if ever 1395
there was one.

DIONYSUS Persuasion is insubstantial and has no mind of its own. Choose a heavy line to weigh down your pan. Something big and powerful.

EURIPIDES Let's think. Where, oh where, can I find the right kind of thing?

Third attempt

Dionysus teases Euripides by seeming to help him – with a heroic throw of *dice* (1400), three light-weight scores. Undismayed, Euripides tries his best and is roundly defeated. He still seems none the wiser.

Review of Round 4

A comprehensive victory for Aeschylus. It is conventional for Greek victors to taunt the defeated, and Aeschylus concludes his triumph by suggesting that Euripides and his works have no gravity. He adds insult to injury by making Euripides a cuckold with mention of Euripides' wife and Cephisophon (see 944). For books, see 53n.

Dionysus' confusion

Dionysus came down to the underworld because of his passion for Euripides (67). He is now not so sure: **One I consider clever, the other I enjoy** (1413) and **One speaks cleverly, the other clearly** (1435). It's not as easy as it was at 822–9 or 901–4 to tell who's who.

● Who *is* who in lines 1413 and 1435?

Pluto

The final character to appear in the play is a sort of *deus ex machina* figure and, indeed, he may literally have appeared *ex machina* (see **'Surprise'**, p. 94) or using the *ekkyklēma* (see **'Reunion'**, p. 20). Pluto (see 162n) grants the release of one or other poet with no conditions attached, unlike Orpheus, who could take Eurydice provided he didn't look back, or Persephone (see **'Demeter'**, p. 28), who could return to Demeter provided she'd eaten nothing in the underworld. Dionysus is encouraged to make his final decision and adopts a simple and sensible method, asking the poets for advice on two important issues of the day.

Agōn: Round 5, political question 1: what to do about Alcibiades

(For Alcibiades' career, see *Background to the story*, pp. v–vii.) Alcibiades was now in his mid-40s. His 1st-century AD biographer Plutarch describes the atmosphere later in Athens, in 404 BC, just after her defeat by Sparta and the imposition of the Thirty Tyrants: *In despair they recalled their past mistakes and follies, and they considered the greatest of all had been their second outburst against Alcibiades... the finest and most experienced general they possessed. And yet in the midst of all their trouble, a faint glimmer of hope remained, that the cause of Athens could never be utterly lost so long as Alcibiades was alive.*

The Spartans ordered their commander Lysander to have him killed: *whether they, too, had become alarmed at his energy and enterprise, or whether they were trying to gratify King Agis* (Plutarch, *Life of Alcibiades* 38).

● Who gives the better response, Euripides or Aeschylus? Why?

DIONYSUS I've got one.

Achilles cast . . . his dice – two ones and a four. 1400

Speak up, then. This is the last round.

EURIPIDES *In his right hand he took a wooden cudgel*
Weighted with iron.

AESCHYLUS *Chariot on chariot, corpse on corpse.*

DIONYSUS He's got the better of you. Again.

EURIPIDES How?

DIONYSUS He put in two chariots and a couple of corpses. Not 1405
even a hundred Egyptians could shift that lot.

AESCHYLUS Instead of doing this line by line, let him hop in and sit
in the pan himself with his children, his wife, Cephisophon, and
all his books. I will speak just two words of my own. 1410

DIONYSUS Good friends, I won't judge them. I won't antagonise
either. One I consider clever, the other I enjoy.

PLUTO Then you won't achieve what you came for.

DIONYSUS And if I do reach a decision? 1415

PLUTO You may take whoever you prefer back with you, so that
your visit isn't wasted.

DIONYSUS Lovely. Well, then, listen to me. I came down for a poet.
Why? So that the city could be saved and put on plays. Whoever
seems most likely to give useful advice to the city, he's the one I 1420
think I should take. So my first question concerns Alcibiades.
What advice does each of you have about him? The city's in a
mess.

AESCHYLUS And what's its view?

DIONYSUS The city's? It longs for him. It detests him. But it wants 1425
to keep him. Tell us, both of you, what you think about him.

EURIPIDES I hate a man who's slow to aid his country
but quick to cause deep harm; good at helping himself, but not at
helping the city.

DIONYSUS By Poseidon, that's good. What's your opinion? 1430

AESCHYLUS One shouldn't raise a lion cub in the city.
But once it's grown, you'd better treat it well.

DIONYSUS By Zeus the saviour, I can't decide.
One speaks cleverly, the other clearly. 1435

Agōn: Round 5, question 2: how to keep Athens safe
Euripides' response

The text is very uncertain at this point in the play, perhaps because it was performed more than once, but Euripides sounds barely coherent and Dionysus has become dismissive. The rejected lines below go a step further and make him ridiculous.

Eu	If someone gave Cleocritus Cinesias' wings, to lift him on the breeze over the sea's smooth surface	1437
Di	It would be ridiculous. What's your point?	
Eu	If he fought in a sea-battle, and took vinegar, he could pour it in the eyes of the enemy.	1440
Di	Bravo, Palamedes. What a genius. Your idea, or Cephisophon's?	1451
Eu	All mine, except the vinegar. That was Cephisophon.	

Cleocritus is thought to be a fat man, possibly an official connected with the Mysteries. **Palamedes** is the Greek who outwitted Odysseus and got him to Troy.

Aeschylus' response

Aeschylus begins cautiously, with a question, as at 1424. He doesn't give his final answer until 1463–5 and then it is enigmatic, like an oracular response. He emphasises the navy, as Themistocles had done, and supports Pericles' policy, which had been to attack the Peloponnese, withdraw into the city and accept the loss of Attica temporarily. His earlier remark on **cloak** and **goatskin** (1459) – town and country – like his image of Alcibiades as lion cub, implies that the Athenians must work together and not let any faction dominate.

- How clear and distinct is the advice of the two poets?
- Why might the audience prefer Aeschylus (1475)?

1466 jurors Juror's pay (3 obols a day) drained the Athenian treasury.

Decision

Dionysus keeps his audience in suspense until line 1471, but Euripides has already sensed which way the wind is blowing and begins his protest. When Dionysus says **I'm relieved** (1481), the Greek literally suggests the lifting of a burden.

- Do you think Dionysus makes the right choice? Why?

DIONYSUS Just one more question for you both about our city and
how to keep her safe.

EURIPIDES I know. I'd like to answer this.   1440

DIONYSUS Go on.

EURIPIDES When we trust what we now mistrust, and when we
mistrust what we now trust...

DIONYSUS What? I don't understand. Could you express that a   1445
little more clearly, for one with a little less learning?

EURIPIDES If we didn't trust the citizens we trust now, but used
those we currently reject...

DIONYSUS We'd be saved.

EURIPIDES If our current misfortune is down to them, mightn't we   1450
find salvation by doing the exact opposite?

DIONYSUS What about you, then? What do you say?

AESCHYLUS First tell me this: who does the city listen to today?   1455
Men of honour?

DIONYSUS Oh no. It hates them most of all.

AESCHYLUS And it likes the wicked?

DIONYSUS Of course not, but it is forced to use them.

AESCHYLUS How can anyone save a city like that, when it rejects
both the cloak and the goatskin?

DIONYSUS You'd better find out, if you want to get back up there.   1460

AESCHYLUS And if I were there, I would tell you. Down here, I'd
rather not.

DIONYSUS Don't be like that. Send your good advice up from
below.

AESCHYLUS When they consider the enemy's land as their own;
their own land as the enemy's; when their ships show the way, a
way that shows there is no other way.   1465

DIONYSUS Yes, but the jurors alone drain what we've got.

PLUTO Please make your decision.

DIONYSUS I'll use the same criterion for each of you.
My heart will make my choice.

EURIPIDES Remember the gods! You swore you'd pick me and take
me back home. Choose your friends.   1470

DIONYSUS *It was my tongue that swore.* I'll take Aeschylus.

EURIPIDES What are you doing, you lousy shit?

Review of the character of Euripides

Dionysus taunts Euripides with the latter's notorious and amoral line: **it was my tongue that swore** (*Hippolytus* 612), a line he earlier professed to love even if he couldn't remember it (100–1). He mocks Euripides' use of facile aphorisms (1477, see 1082). This is a matter of life and death for Euripides, even though he appears very ungracious in defeat.

● Do you feel sorry for Euripides, or does he get what he deserves? Are the Chorus too harsh in lines 1491–9?

Chorus' verdict

The Chorus approve the choice. They devote one verse to praising Aeschylus for his understanding and end with one that sums up Euripides' weaknesses.

1492 Socrates This is the only direct mention of Socrates in the play, but there has been significant overlap between themes in this play and in *Clouds*, the play that satirises Socrates' teachings. Euripides and Socrates were both seen by some contemporaries as undermining old-fashioned values, in particular religious and moral values. Socrates quickly became a martyr for independent thinkers and (excepting Socrates' attack on **the arts**, 1493, in Plato, *Republic* 10) 21st-century verdicts on both these figures have been kinder.

EXODOS (1500–33)

Comedy at the festival of Dionysus usually ended, appropriately, with revels and a party atmosphere. Pluto is the host, generously offering the means of reaching his realm early (**this/these** are knives, nooses or the like) to some of the undesirables on earth. Little is known of **Myrmex and Nicomachus** (1506) or **Archenomos** (1507).

1504 Cleophon (see *Background to the story*, pp. v–vii, 140n, 678n and 1532). Diodorus Siculus, a 1st-century BC historian, writes of Cleophon's crucial role in rejecting peace in 410 BC as follows (13.53):

Cleophon, the most influential leader of the populace at this time, taking the floor and arguing at length on the question in his own fashion, buoyed up the people, citing the magnitude of their military successes ... Consequently the Athenians, after taking unwise counsel, repented of it when it could do them no good, and, deceived as they were by words spoken in flattery, they made a blunder so vital that never again at any time were they able truly to recover.

Curiously, Xenophon mentions him only once in his account of the closing years of the war, on the occasion of his execution in 404 BC.

DIONYSUS Me? I've decided Aeschylus is the winner. Why not?

EURIPIDES Can you look me in the eye after this outrage?

DIONYSUS An outrage? That's not what the audience think.   1475

EURIPIDES You bastard. Will you stand there and see me dead?

DIONYSUS *Who knows if life is death, or breathing feeding, or sleep a*
sheep?

PLUTO Please step inside, Dionysus.

DIONYSUS What for?

PLUTO So we can entertain you both before you sail back.   1480

DIONYSUS Good idea, by Zeus. I'm relieved at the outcome.

CHORUS OF INITIATES Blessed is the man
Who's quick to understand
And learns in many ways.
Here's one who's got some sense, it seems,   1485
Who's off back home again.
A good thing for the citizens,
A good thing for himself, his friends, his family
Because he understands.   1490

Refinement doesn't mean
Sitting with Socrates in idle chatter,
Throwing out the arts,
And ignoring the greatness
Of the tragedian's craft.
The man who wastes his time   1495
In idle talk on pompous,
Petty quibbles is deranged.

PLUTO So then, Aeschylus, go happily on your way   1500
and save our city with your good advice.
Educate those fools – and there are quite a few!
Take this and give it to Cleophon,
and give these to those bankers   1505
Myrmex and Nicomachus;
this is for Archenomus.
Tell them to get down here fast
– no lingering. And if they don't hurry up,   1510

1514 Adeimantus An aristocrat who, like Alcibiades, fled Athens when accused of involvement in the profanation of the Mysteries (p. 32). He returned to a command in the Athenian navy and escaped Pluto's grasp for longer than might have been expected.

1515 Sophocles See note on p. 54.

1518 in case I end up here again Aeschylus is uncertain whether he is undergoing some sort of apotheosis, but there are elements of hero-cult worship in the bringing out of holy torches.

A final prayer
The final prayer is for Athens and her safety. This was a frightening and uncertain time for the city, and worse was to come in the months ahead, with an end to war but crushing terms for Athens and her democratic institutions.

By Apollo, I'll brand them,
Bind them hand and foot
And dispatch them underground fast
Along with Leucolophus' son, Adeimantus.

AESCHYLUS I'll do so. In return, give my chair to Sophocles   1515
To watch over and keep safe
In case I end up here again some day.
For I judge that in wisdom he takes second place.   1520
And see to it that that good for nothing, lying thief
Never sits in my seat, even by mistake.

PLUTO Bring out the holy torches for Aeschylus   1525
And send him on his way celebrating out loud
With his own songs and dances.

CHORUS OF INITIATES Gods who dwell below the earth,
Grant this poet a good journey
As he sets out on his return to the light.
Grant the city good advice that brings great benefits.   1530
May our great troubles,
Our destructive use of arms
End completely.
Let Cleophon,
And anyone else who wants to,
Fight in their own native land.

Synopsis of the play

PROLOGUE (1–315)

1–37 Dionysus and Xanthias: embarking on a journey Dionysus appears on stage dressed as a parody of Heracles, together with a slave, weighed down by baggage, and a donkey. After a stand-up routine about not making the audience laugh with old, familiar baggage jokes, Dionysus reveals that he is on his way to Heracles for advice on a journey to the underworld.

38–165 Advice from Heracles Dionysus tells Heracles that he wants to go there to bring back Euripides because there are no good poets still alive. His appearance and plan cause Heracles great amusement and he teases Dionysus with his advice. He tells him what to expect.

166–208 Negotiating the passage across the marsh After a brief encounter with a corpse who refuses to take all the baggage, Dionysus crosses the marsh on Charon's boat. Charon makes Xanthias take the long way round.

209–70 Encounter with frogs On the journey, a subsidiary Chorus of Frogs engage in a short singing contest with Dionysus as Charon makes him row across.

271–315 Dionysus and Xanthias reunited After Dionysus and Xanthias are reunited on the other side, they encounter a shape-changing monster. Dionysus is seen to be a coward. They hear the Chorus of Initiates approaching.

PARODOS (316–459)

The Initiates of the Eleusinian Mysteries enter. They invoke Iacchus to come and join them in their celebration, consisting of dancing and burning torches. They then sing a warning to those not initiated to keep clear, and add some ritual abuse. After a hymn praising Demeter, they indulge in some more ritual insults and rude political abuse. Dionysus and Xanthias join in with this and they all end up outside Hades' palace.

EPISODES: PRELIMINARY ENCOUNTERS IN THE UNDERWORLD (460–674)

Hades' doorman (460–502) The doorman, Aeacus, answers Dionysus' knocking. Mistaking him for the real Heracles who had kidnapped the dog Cerberus on his earlier visit, Aeacus verbally attacks Dionysus. The god is so scared that he forces Xanthias to change clothes with him to avoid the attack.

The maid (504–33) Straight after they have done this, a maid comes out of the palace. She had fancied Heracles on his previous visit and has prepared a gourmet dinner and arranged dancing girls for him.

Dionysus is eager to sample these delights and so he forces Xanthias to change clothes again.

The Chorus (534–48) The Chorus reflect on changes of plan in general.

The innkeepers (549–88) Two women emerge from an inn. They are enraged because Heracles, well known for his gluttony, had eaten an enormous amount of food on his previous visit. Dionysus pleads with Xanthias to exchange clothes a third time so that his slave can bear the brunt of the women's attack.

The Chorus (589–604) They encourage Xanthias, who is currently disguised as Dionysus.

Revenge of the doorman (605–74) Aeacus returns with his thugs to punish 'Heracles' (actually Xanthias). Xanthias seeks to deflect the beating by offering his 'slave' (Dionysus, in Xanthias' own clothes) for torture. Both are beaten to see who is telling the truth, on the grounds that the one who is a god would not feel pain. The beatings do not give a decisive answer.

PARABASIS (675–737)
After invoking the Muse, the Chorus give their views on topical issues. The main themes are: all citizens should be treated as equals, rights for the generals put on trial after the Battle of Arginusae, the similarities between the debasement of military leadership and coinage.

EPISODES: THE AGŌN (738–1499)
Slave talk (738–813) Xanthias chats to a fellow slave about their respective masters and the forthcoming contest. Aeschylus holds the throne of tragedy, but Euripides has recently arrived and is claiming the position. He is well supported by crooks, of which Hades is full. A contest of their poetry is going to be held and the inhabitants of the underworld are looking to Dionysus to be judge since he is god of drama.

First appearances (814–74) The Chorus anticipate the appearance of Euripides and Aeschylus. The two tragedians hurl initial insults at each other.

Agōn: opening prayers (875–94) The Chorus invoke the Muses; Aeschylus swears by the traditional Olympian gods; Euripides swears by his own new gods.

Agōn: prelude (895–906) The Chorus express their eagerness for the contest to start.

Agōn: Round 1 Taking the lead, Euripides **(907–91)** criticises the overblown writing style of Aeschylus and the way he treats his audience, particularly at the opening of his plays. He praises his own clarity and focus on scenarios with which his audience can engage. Dionysus adds his own commentary, as he does in each round. The Chorus encourage Aeschylus to reply (**992–1006**).

Aeschylus (**1007–98**) points out that his characters are noble and good role-models and that he teaches useful things, as poets before him have done. Euripides, in contrast, has given many examples of unsuitable and unseemly behaviour, such as dressing his noble characters in rags. The Chorus comment (**1099–1118**) that the contest is evenly matched: the audience is not ignorant and can follow arguments either may make.

***Agōn*: Round 2**   Each poet criticises the prologues (opening sections) of the other. Euripides' attacks on Aeschylus consist of making verbal quibbles about the content. He takes examples from five lines of one of Aeschylus' plays (**1119–77**).

Aeschylus starts off by criticising Euripides' choice of words, but soon changes course by parodying the rhythm and predictability of his rival's verse, quoting the opening lines of several plays (**1177–1248**) and finishing them all with a reference to a 'little bottle'.

***Agōn*: Round 3**   They parody each other's lyric (sung) style. Euripides is again the first to speak (**1249–1304**), criticising the predictability of Aeschylus and his use of refrains. He then parodies Aeschylus' style of solo song.

In response, Aeschylus parodies Euripides' music and his banal content, unworthy of tragedy (**1305–63**).

***Agōn*: Round 4 (1364–1410)**   Aeschylus proposes taking Euripides across to the scales; the Chorus express their surprise at this method of judging. Dionysus starts to take a more active role, getting each to quote one line from their own play into the pan. Aeschylus wins this round decisively – each time his line is heavier.

***Agōn*: Round 5 (1411–81)**   Pluto (Hades) makes it clear that Dionysus has to judge between them, but that he can indeed take the winning poet back with him. Dionysus asks each poet two questions designed to get advice that will be useful to Athens. The first question asks what Athens should think about Alcibiades (who had had a very chequered career, including defecting for a while to Sparta). The second asks how Athens should be kept safe. In a reversal of his stated reason for visiting the underworld, Dionysus chooses Aeschylus. Euripides is outraged. Pluto invites Dionysus inside his palace.

Chorus (1482–99)   Aeschylus has shown true wisdom, while Euripides has indulged in petty quibbles.

EXODOS (1500–33)

On their return, Pluto wishes Aeschylus well as he returns to save the city and educate the citizens and lists those Athenian politicians he wants to see soon. Aeschylus says that Sophocles can be his deputy and have the chair of tragedy – Euripides is definitely not allowed to sit in it. The Chorus wish Aeschylus a happy return journey and hope for peace in Athens.

Introduction to the Greek Theatre

Theātron, the Greek word that gave us 'theatre' in English, meant both 'viewing place' and the assembled viewers. These ancient viewers (*theātai*) were in some ways very different from their modern counterparts. For a start, they were participants in a religious festival, and they went to watch plays only on certain days in the year, when shows were put on in honour of Dionysus. At Athens, where drama developed many of its most significant traditions, the main Dionysus festival, held in the spring, was one of the most important events in the city's calendar, attracting large numbers of citizens and visitors from elsewhere in the Greek world. It is not known for certain whether women attended; if any did, they were more likely to be visitors than the wives of Athenian citizens.

The festival was also a great sporting occasion. Performances designed to win the god's favour needed spectators to witness and share in the event, just as the athletic contests did at Olympia or Delphi, and one of the ways in which the spectators got involved was through competition. What they saw were three sets of three tragedies plus a satyr play, five separate comedies and as many as twenty song-and-dance performances called dithyrambs, put on in honour of Dionysus by choruses representing the different 'tribes' into which the citizen body was divided. There was a contest for each different event, with the dithyramb choruses divided into men's and boys' competitions, and a panel of judges determined the winners. The judges were appointed to act on behalf of the city; no doubt they took some notice of the way the audience responded on each occasion. Attendance at these events was on a large scale: we should be thinking of football crowds rather than typical theatre audiences in the modern world.

Like football matches, dramatic festivals were open-air occasions, and the performances were put on in daylight rather than with stage lighting in a darkened auditorium. The ideal performance space in these circumstances was a hollow hillside to seat spectators, with a flat area at the bottom (*orchēstra*) in which the chorusmen could spread out for their dancing and singing and which could be closed off by a stage-building (*skēnē*) acting simultaneously as backdrop, changing room and sounding board. Effective acoustics and good sight-lines were achieved by the kind of design represented in Fig. A on page 109, the theatre of Dionysus at Athens. The famous stone theatre at Epidaurus (Fig. B), built about 330 BC, and often taken as typical, has a circular *orchēstra*, but in the fifth century it was normal practice for theatres to have a low wooden stage in front of the *skēnē*, for use by the actors, who also interacted with the chorus in the *orchēstra*.

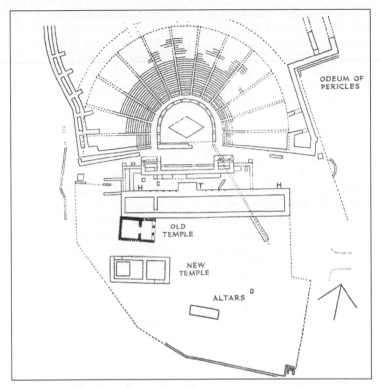

Fig. A. The theatre of Dionysus at Athens.

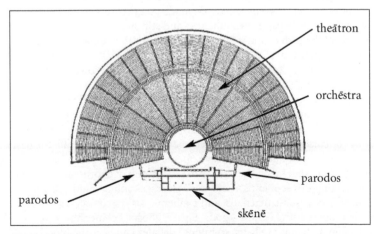

Fig. B. The theatre at Epidaurus (fourth century BC).

Song and dance by choruses and the accompanying music of the piper were integral to all these types of performance and not just to the dithyramb. In tragedy there were 12 (later 15) chorusmen, in comedy 24, and in dithyramb 50; plays were often named after their chorus: Aeschylus' *Persians*, Euripides' *Bacchae*, Aristophanes' *Birds* are familiar examples. The rhythmic movements, groupings and singing of the chorus contributed crucially to the overall impact of each show, ensuring that there was always an animated stage picture even when only one or two actors were in view. The practice of keeping the number of speaking actors normally restricted to three, with doubling of roles by the same actor where necessary, looks odd at first sight, but it makes sense in the special circumstance of Greek theatrical performance. Two factors are particularly relevant: first the use of masks, which was probably felt to be fundamental to shows associated with the cult of Dionysus and which made it easy for an actor to take more than one part within a single play, and second the need to concentrate the audience's attention by keeping the number of possible speakers limited. In a large, open acting area some kind of focusing device is important if the spectators are always to be sure where to direct their gaze. The Greek plays that have survived, particularly the tragedies, are extremely economical in their design, with no sub-plots or complications in the action which audiences might find distracting or confusing. Acting style, too, seems to have relied on large gestures and avoidance of fussy detail; we know from the size of some of the surviving theatres that many spectators would be sitting too far away to catch small-scale gestures or stage business. Some plays make powerful use of props, like Ajax's sword, Philoctetes' bow, or the head of Pentheus in *Bacchae*, but all these are carefully chosen to be easily seen and interpreted.

Above all, actors seem to have depended on their highly trained voices in order to captivate audiences and stir their emotions. By the middle of the fifth century there was a prize for the best actor in the tragic competition, as well as for the playwright and the financial sponsor of the performance (*chorēgos*), and comedy followed suit a little later. What was most admired in the leading actors who were entitled to compete for this prize was the ability to play a series of different and very demanding parts in a single day and to be a brilliant singer as well as a compelling speaker of verse: many of the main parts involve solo songs or complex exchanges between actor and chorus. Overall, the best plays and performances must have offered audiences a great charge of energy and excitement: the chance to see a group of chorusmen dancing and singing in a sequence of different guises, as young maidens, old counsellors, ecstatic maenads, and exuberant satyrs; to watch scenes in which supernatural beings – gods, Furies, ghosts – come into contact with human beings; to listen to intense debates and hear the blood-curdling offstage cries that heralded the arrival of a messenger with an account of terrifying deeds within, and then to see the bodies brought out and witness the lamentations. Far more 'happened' in most plays than we can easily imagine from the bare text on the page; this must help to account for the continuing appeal of drama throughout antiquity and across the Greco-Roman world.

From the fourth century onwards dramatic festivals became popular wherever there were communities of Greek speakers, and other gods besides Dionysus were honoured with performances of plays. Actors, dancers and musicians organised themselves for professional touring – some of them achieved star status and earned huge fees – and famous old plays were revived as part of the repertoire. Some of the plays that had been first performed for Athenian citizens in the fifth century became classics for very different audiences – women as well as men, Latin speakers as well as Greeks – and took on new kinds of meaning in their new environment. But theatre was very far from being an antiquarian institution: new plays, new dramatic forms like mime and pantomime, changes in theatre design, staging, masks and costumes all demonstrate its continuing vitality in the Hellenistic and Roman periods. Nearly all the Greek plays that have survived into modern times are ones that had a long theatrical life in antiquity; this perhaps helps to explain why modern actors, directors and audiences have been able to rediscover their power.

For further reading: entries in *Oxford Classical Dictionary* (3rd edition) under 'theatre staging, Greek' and 'comedy (Greek), Old'; J.R. Green, 'The theatre', Ch. 7 of *The Cambridge Ancient History, Plates to Volumes V and VI*, Cambridge, 1994; Richard Green and Eric Handley, *Images of the Greek Theatre*, London, 1995.

Pat Easterling

Time line

The events of the Peloponnesian War between 431 and 404 BC are an important background to *Frogs*. The Spartans had the edge in their effectiveness on the battlefield, but the Athenians had the better navy (both more numerous and better trained). The combination of effective control of the sea and the Long Walls, protecting the route between the port of Piraeus and the city centre, meant that the Athenians could withstand the invasion of their territory by shipping in food by sea, even after the Spartans established a permanent presence in Attica. The Athenian fleet was completely destroyed at the Battle of Aegospotami in 405, and by March of 404 Athens was forced to surrender, on humiliating terms, to Sparta.

Date BC		Other events
c. 525	Aeschylus born	
c. 496	Sophocles born	
490		**First Persian invasion:** Battle of Marathon
486	Comedy first allowed at the Dionysia	
c. 480	Euripides born	**Second Persian invasion:** Battles of Thermopylae and Salamis (479)
472	*Persians* (Aeschylus)	
458	*Oresteia* – last plays of Aeschylus	
c. 456	Aeschylus dies	
c. 460–450	Aristophanes born	
438	*Telephus* (Euripides) play not survived	
431	*Medea* (Euripides)	Outbreak of Peloponnesian War between Athens and Sparta
428	*Hippolytus* (Euripides)	
427	Banqueters	
426	***Babylonians***	
425	***Acharnians***	
424	***Knights***	
422	***Wasps***	
421	***Peace***	**Peace of Nicias**
418	***Clouds*** (revised)	
415	*Heracles* (Euripides) approximate date	Resumption of full-scale hostilities. **Sicilian Expedition** strongly argued for by Alcibiades in the Athenian assembly. After the Mutilation of the Herms, Alcibiades defects to Sparta.

Date BC		Other events
414	*Birds*	
413		Sparta occupies Decelea 20 km from Athens all year round, cutting off food supplies by land and disrupting the Athenian economy
412	*Andromeda* (Euripides)	
411	*Lysistrata* *Thesmophoriazousae*	Suspension of democracy in Athens with rule by oligarchs (the Four Hundred). They are encouraged by Alcibiades, who suggests he may be able to bring the Persian fleet in on the side of the Athenians.
410		Restoration of democracy in Athens. Defeat of Spartans at the **Battle of Cyzicus.**
408	Wealth	
407		Alcibiades returns to Athens after military success and starts taking part in political life again. He leads the first procession to Eleusis since the occupation of Decelea.
406	Euripides dies. Sophocles dies winter 406/405. *Frogs* written and rehearsed	**Battle of Notium** – Athenian navy, under the command of Alcibiades, suffers a significant defeat and he goes into voluntary exile. Defeat of Spartans at **Battle of Arginusae**, but Athenian generals are put on trial for failing to rescue their dead and injured.
405	*Frogs* performed in January. Phrynichus' *Muses* comes second. *Bacchae* (Euripides)	Athenian fleet destroyed at the **Battle of Aegospotami** in August.
404		Athens forced to surrender in March. Sparta installs Oligarchy of the Thirty (nobles sympathetic to Sparta and its values) and orders the walls to be pulled down.
401	*Oedipus at Colonus* (Sophocles)	
392	*Ecclesiazousae*	
388	*Wealth II*	
c. 386	Aristophanes dies	

This table includes all the surviving plays of Aristophanes and those of the other tragedians to which reference is made. However, some plays and surviving fragments cannot be accurately dated.

Index

Achilles 62, 86
Adeimantus 32, 102
Aeacus 34, 42
Aegeus 48
Aegyptus 82
Aeschylus vi, 52, 64, 68
afterlife 10; *see also* underworld
Agamemnon 62, 76, 78, 88
Agathon 6
agōns (competitions) vi, 48, 56, 60
Alcibiades v–vi, 24, 32, 50, 96
Alcmene 38
Ameipsias 2
Andocides 32
Anthesteria (Festival of Flowers) 16
Aphrodite 72
Archedemus 30, 42
Arginusae sea-battle v, 4, 38, 50
Athens: democracy v, 66, 102; map x; safety 98, 102; theatre of Dionysus 108, 109
Attica ix
audience interaction 20, 22

balance/scales 54, 92, 94
bathos 44, 82, 90
burial of dead 12

Cadmus 84
Callias 32, 36
centaurs 4
Cephisophon 64
Ceramicus 10
Cerberus vi, 8, 10, 12, 34
Charon 14, 16
choruses 8, 16, 24, 48, 110
chthonic *see* underworld
Cinesias 12, 26
cithara 88
classes in society/military 14
Cleidemides 54

Cleigenes 50
Cleisthenes 4, 32
Cleitophon 66
Cleocritus 98
Cleon 40
Cleophon v, 10, 48, 100
clothes 4, 34, 36, 40, 74
Clouds vi, 54, 60, 100
Cocytus river 34
coins 50; *see also* money
comedy *see* humour
Corinth 32
craft 54
Cratinus 26
Cretans 92
Critias 32

dancing 24, 38, 88, 110
Darius 70
Day of Pots 16
dead, burial 12
death vi, 6, 10, 70
Delos 48
Delphi 48
Demeter 4, 10, 24, 26, 28, 60
democracy v, 66, 102
Dictynna 92
diet 64
Dionysus vi; family 2, 6, 42; festivals vi, 2, 16, 30, 108; image 18, 38, 82
disguise/dressing up 4, 34, 36, 40, 74
dramatic festivals vi, 2, 30, 108

Echidna 34
Eleusinian Mysteries 10, 22, 24–32
Empusa 22
Epidaurus theatre 108, 109
Erasinides v, 82
Eryxix 64

Euripides vi, 6, 54, 58, 62, 100
exclusion from the Mysteries 26, 28
Exodus 100

festivals of Dionysus vi, 2, 16, 30, 108
fitness 74
flower festival (Anthesteria) 16
flutes *see* pipe music
frog chorus 16, 18

gods 2, 4, 38, 78; *see also individual gods and goddesses*
Gorgons 34
Greek theatres 108–111

Hades (Pluto) vi, 12, 28, 96, 100
Hecate 22, 26, 92
Hegelochus 22
hemlock 10
Heracles vi, 4, 8, 34, 36, 40
Hermes 78
Hesiod 70
Hipponax 48
Hipponicus 32
Homer 10, 28, 56, 70, 80
homosexuality 4, 90
housekeeping 68
hubris 2
humour 2, 14, 20, 28, 58
Hyperbolus 40

Iacchus 24, 30
Initiates of the Mysteries 10, 24
innkeepers 40
invented words 18, 66, 72
Iophon 6

justice 54

Lamachus 72
Lesbian 90
Lethargy 14
Lycis 2

lyric passages 18, 48, 58, 86

male and female virtue 72
maps ix–x
Marathon 52, 70, 88
Megaenetus 66
Meletides 66
military classes 14, 70
modern performances of the Frogs 18, 46
money v, 10, 12, 50, 98
monodies 90
Morsimus 12
Musaeus 70
Muses 60, 90
music 24, 86
mysteries *see* Eleusinian Mysteries

names 40, 44, 92
navy v, 14, 50, 74, 112
Niobe 62
Nysian 16

oaths 4, 42
Odysseus 10, 20, 62, 80, 98
Odyssey (Homer) 10, 20, 34, 74, 80
Oedipus 54, 70, 82
Oeneus 84
Oresteia 76
Orestes 78
Orpheus vi, 12, 28, 70

paedophilia 4
Palamedes 98
Panathenaea 12, 74
parabasis 48, 52
parodos 24–32, 62
Patroclus 72
Peloponnesian War (Sparta) v–vi, 4, 70, 100, 102, 112–113
Pelops 84
Persephone 10, 26
Persian wars 52, 70, 88
Phaedra 72
Phormisius 66

Phrynichus 2, 48, 62, 88
pig sacrifice 24, 26
pine torches 24
pipe music 24, 86, 88, 110
Plataea 50
Pluto (Hades) vi, 12, 28, 96, 100
poetic contests vi, 6, 18; *see also*
    agōns
poets vi, 6, 48, 54; *see also*
    individual poets
politicians v, 38, 40, 50
priestesses 86
prizes 6, 110
prologues 76
props 84, 110
puns 14, 22, 30, 32
Pythangelos 6

reading books 53, 64, 76
rowing 14

sacrifices 24, 26, 58
Salamis 16
saviour 28
scales/balance 54, 92, 94
scapegoats 52
sea-battle v, 4, 38, 50
singing 18, 24, 110
slaves v, 4, 44, 52, 66
social classes 14, 70
Socrates 100, 102
solo performances 90, 110
Sondheim adaptation 18, 46
sophists vi, 8, 60, 70, 76, 80
Sophocles vi, 54, 82

Sparta *see* Peloponnesian War
special effects 20, 94, 96
stage directions 24, 46
staging the play 2, 16, 20, 94
Stheneboea 72
storms 58
swan frogs 16
synopsis 104–107

Tantalus 84
taxation 4, 8, 26
Telephus 58
Teucer 72
theatres 22, 108–111
Theramenes 38, 66
Theseus 10
Thorycion 26, 28
thunderer 56, 58
time line 112–113
torch-races 10, 12, 74
torture 44
triremes 74

underworld vi, 10, 78

virtue 72
visual art 64

wars *see* Peloponnesian War;
    Persian wars
weather v, 58
women 26, 38, 66, 68, 72

Xanthias 20
Xenocles 6

Acknowledgements

The authors and publishers acknowledge the following sources of copyright material and are grateful for the permissions granted. While every effort has been made, it has not always been possible to identify the sources of all the material used, or to trace all copyright holders. If any omissions are brought to our notice, we will be happy to include the appropriate acknowledgements on reprinting.

Cover Caia images/Alamy; p. 8 Archaic Ionian Hydria depicting Heracles Bringing Cerberus to Eurystheus, from Cerveteri, c.530 BC (pottery), Greek, (6th century BC) / Louvre, Paris, France / The Bridgeman Art Library; p. 12 Ivy Close Images/Alamy; p. 16 Attic white-ground lekythos decorated with Charon, the ferryman of the Underworld receiving the soul of a dead person, from Athens, c.475–425 BC (ceramic), Tymbos Painter (fl.c.475–450 BC) / Ashmolean Museum, University of Oxford, UK / The Bridgeman Art Library; pp. 18, 46 Photo by Drew Yenchak, with thanks to Point Park University's Pittsburgh Playhouse; p. 20 Moviestore Collection Ltd/ Alamy; p. 40 The Art Archive/Archaeological Museum Ferrara/ Collection Dagli Orti; p. 50 Emergency stater of Athens, 406 BC, Struck, Gold; 8.58g, Harvard Art Museums/Arthur M. Sackler Museums/ Arthur M. Sackler Museum, loan from the Trustees of the Arthur Stone Dewing Greek Numismatic Foundation, 1.1965.1624. Photo: Imaging Department © President and Fellows of Harvard College; pp. 62, 88 © The Trustees of the British Museum; p. 74 Small Panathenaic Amphora, Bulas Group, Athens (ceramic), Greek School, (4th century BC) / © Czartoryski Museum, Cracow, Poland / The Bridgeman Art Library